Jean Walton

Everyday Girl
ADVENTURES

Jaime
Oberlubbesing

A Collection of Everyday
Stories Told by Everyday Girls

Jean Walton

Founder of Everyday Girl Adventures and
MissFit Networking Group

Everyday girl. Optimistic realist. Adventure
enthusiast. Self-proclaimed superhero.

Jean's flair for adventure and passion for life are no secret to those who meet her. She sees the joy in the smallest moments and finds the silver lining in even the worst of situations. But if you ask her, she would tell you that most of her joy comes from sharing experiences with those around her and creating memories that last a lifetime.

Growing up in a large, artistic and musical family, Jean spent much of her life feeling stuck in the background. She always had a passion for adventure and would often accompany her family in their endeavors. She knew she wanted something more but lacked the confidence to feel she ever could be anything more than the average Clark Kent. However, when Jean found herself starting over in life, divorced after a 17-year marriage, with three grown kids and a day job that lost its luster, she finally decided that just existing wasn't enough. She realized she was the only one who could make her dreams a reality. So she straightened her tiara, put on her cape, and set out to become her own superhero.

So began Everyday Girl Adventures. Born from the nostalgia of fun experiences she had with her family and girlfriends, Jean's brand seeks and organizes fun and unique opportunities to bring people together and create lasting memories. Adventure is everywhere. Jean's goal is to help others recognize the joy of a moment and inspire them to find the adventure in their everyday.

Having spent most of her life feeling like a misfit herself, Jean also wanted to create a place where entrepreneurs of all backgrounds could feel comfortable coming together, no matter the stage of their business, to inspire each other and grow their businesses. Jean understands the universal connection women have with one another and the empowerment that comes from women supporting women. MissFit Networking Group is a place for just that—it's where every "miss" fits.

When people ask how Jean manages to have so many fun experiences, the answer is simple: she says yes to every opportunity. You only live once—and ultimately, it's the memories, no matter how big or small, that make it all worth living. So, say yes to every opportunity. Find your superpower. Believe in your dreams. In the end, we only regret the chances we didn't take.

Acknowledgements

My mom, Maggie—for instilling me with a sense of adventure and encouraging me through a "say yes" mentality to every opportunity that arises. Even seemingly mundane moments can become magical with the right attitude.

My daughter Reese—for being willing to go along with all my silly ideas and inspiring Mother/Daughter Mondays.

My sister, Christina—for inspiring me to "Aim Higher" every day.

My partners in fun, Jaime and Teresa—for joining me on this journey to create special moments with the hope of inspiring others.

And my other sisters, Kelly, Margie and Mary and all of my friends—for being the people in my life that not only support me in everything I do but inspire me to create memories through our everyday adventures.

Adventure Atlas

Preface

Destination 1.....Adventures of a "Miss"Fit Entrepreneur 15

Destination 2.....Adventures of a "Miss"chevious Alter Ego. 27

Destination 3....."Miss"led Adventures of Becoming a Mom. 37

Destination 4.....Adventures of a "Miss"tical Traveler. 46

Destination 5.....Adventures of a "Miss"hap-hazard Sourdough Baker. 53

Destination 6.....Adventures of a "Miss"calculated Girl's Night Out. 60

Destination 7.....The Italian Adventures of a "Miss"guided Tourist. 69

Destination 8.....Adventures of a "Miss"aligned Roadtrip. 81

Destination 9.....The "Miss"taken Adventures of Death at the Black Sand Beach. 88

Destination 10.... Adventures of a "Miss"interpreted Life Plan.......................94

Destination 11....Never "Miss" the Opportunity for an Adventure..................................106

Destination 12.... "Miss"cellaneous Adventures of a Solo Explorer................................108

Destination 13.... Adventures of a "Miss"placed Dreamer...115

Destination 14....Adventures of a "Miss"understood Gen-Z........................126

Destination 15.... Adventures of a "Miss"terious Feast of the Senses..............................143

Destination 16....Adventures of a "Mis"-ter's Late Revelation....................................153

Meet the Authors

Preface

There is magic in a memory—

One so strong you can still feel it in the present. When you close your eyes, it paints a canvas right in front of you. So vivid that as you reminisce, you fall right back into time and place. These are the memories you remember for years to come—the moments you find yourself sharing over and over again.

You don't have to lead an extravagant life to find these extraordinary moments. For me it happens all the time. I'm just an everyday girl with small-town roots and a nine-to-five job, but I'd argue that my life is far from ordinary. Why? Because adventure lives in the day-to-day moments we take for granted. It shines in the light of our successes and hides in the shadows of our mistakes. It shows up in the chances we choose to take. When you treat each moment as an adventure, you'll find it everywhere. You just have to be willing to look.

Some of the best memories even come from the worst mistakes. There is something valuable about finding the silver linings. Not to mention, the mishaps along the way sure do make for some fun stories! So, whether you're traveling across the world, embarking on a journey to self-discovery, enjoying a spontaneous day, or recalling the most ridiculous thing that happened to you, everyone has an adventure to share.

Many of my favorite adventures come from the time spent with my mom, my daughter, and my girlfriends over the years. My connections with other women are very prevalent in my life. I value the individual perspectives we each have to offer and wanted to provide an opportunity for other women to share their stories of joy, hope and inspiration. So, I created this book as a collection of stories from everyday women, from all stages and walks of life, sharing a sense of adventure through their unique lenses. Everyday Adventures.

In the end, all we are left with are the memories, so why not make them worth remembering? May you find the fun, laughter and joy in these stories and be inspired to seek the adventure in *your* everyday.

Adventures of a "Miss"Fit Entrepreneur

By Jean Walton

Everyone has a story. Less than a year ago, I didn't think mine was all that significant. But between then and now there have been some interesting developments.

I used to hear the word entrepreneur and think that it meant someone who owned a business and had a lot of money. But when you look up the word entrepreneur, it is defined as, "a person who organizes and operates a business". So, I was wrong on both accounts. You don't have to own a business or have a lot of money to be an entrepreneur. It would seem I had the wrong idea about a lot of things over the years. Despite that, I do get to do a lot of cool things simply because I say yes to every opportunity. Where did it all begin? Well, I have this tendency to do things backwards. But sometimes, the beginning of one thing happens at the end of something else. So, the beginning of my story starts at the end—the end of the old me.

Not long after my divorce, three years ago, I had decided to start saying yes to opportunities. I wanted more fun and adventure in my life and to do the things I never would have tried to do before. This was a big step for me; a milestone of sorts. I've always been kind of a scaredy-cat when it comes to trying anything out of my comfort zone.

You see, when I was younger, I was incredibly shy and scared to do anything that would give people reasons to judge me. I didn't have a lot of confidence and was too afraid to put myself out there. All I wanted to do was just fit in. I spent most of my life trying to be adaptable and blend in with the people around me. I didn't want to be different. I suffered from low self-esteem growing up. Being right in the middle of four sisters and five brothers, I never felt pretty enough or good enough at anything I did.

I'm part Native American. I have olive skin and angular features. And, to me, this meant I was ugly. Most of my siblings are fair-complected. So that makes me different. There was a lot of racism in my hometown towards Native Americans. It didn't feel good when people told me my sisters were pretty, but rarely said anything like that to me. On top of that, my family is very musically and artistically talented. I don't know how that gene managed to escape me. Yet here I am, mediocre at best with my singing abilities, and I can't draw to save my life. I wish I could say that I've overcome this low opinion of myself years later. But it's a constant struggle even to this day.

This probably explains why I married someone who I never felt compatible with. But at the time I felt lucky that I had found someone who wanted to be with a twenty-five-year-old, single mom with a baby. It also explains why I had a baby in the first place, but no lasting relationship with his biological father—not exactly the life I had always dreamed about when I was young and hopeful.

I was married for seventeen years. When you've been married that long, you know you have tried everything you could to make it work. For that, I am absolutely certain. After my divorce, I went on a lot of dates trying to find Mr. Right, Mr. Compatible, Mr. Completes Me. I didn't know what it was like to be in a relationship with someone you considered your best friend. I've always wanted that.

I went on 50ish first dates, truth be told. After a few great starts that resulted in disappointment after disappointment, I finally found him. Or so I thought. What appeared to be a magical first date, common interests, lifestyles that meshed, etc. Looking back, I now realize that the first date actually foreshadowed what happened the two months that followed. Red flags galore. But what did I know? I hadn't exactly been in a successful relationship. Even my marriage was unsuccessful for seventeen long years.

Despite my misgivings, it was Mr. 50th Disappointment who made the decision to end things. I knew it wasn't perfect, but after all the amazing days of feeling like I had finally found someone who fit into my life, I had a really hard time accepting that he wasn't THE ONE. How could someone just turn off their feelings for you and walk away? At the time, I couldn't see that he actually gave me a gift; the gift of opportunity. I didn't realize that it was going to be the pivotal moment in my life where I would decide to do everything different going forward. That is where my story and the adventures begin...

To explain where things went from that point, I have to back up for a moment and give a little background on the range of opportunities and inspirations I am blessed to have.

My sister, Christy, is an astronaut manager. Yep, that is actually a thing. Any public figure needs a manager to organize their speaking engagements and activities. Astronauts are no different. I've been fortunate enough to ride on my sister's coat tails on several occasions to meet some really interesting people and participate in some memorable events. It is inevitable to get inspired and want more out of life being around so many incredible individuals.

When Christy asked me to be an assistant in her space gala project in London in May of 2022, I didn't hesitate to say yes. I just knew it was going to be an amazing opportunity. And it was. Not only did I get to participate in assistant-producing the "Space Oscar's" in LONDON, I had the most epic trip of a lifetime!

The experience was four days of events that started with an exclusive welcome reception for the astronauts and production team and ended with a themed May the 4th

After After party where we all dressed as Star Wars characters. I was a stormtrooper.

A couple of days after the events, everyone else went home and back to their regular lives. I stayed in Europe with the original intent to accompany Christy to some work meetings in Dubai. I've never been to Dubai. It was an exciting opportunity that I couldn't pass up. But plans changed and we went on holiday to Portugal instead. Portugal was a dream come true! We stayed in fancy resorts, got invited on boat rides, and it felt like we were treated like celebrities. The star treatment was courtesy of my sister's luxury travel designer friend, Bex. *Where can I get a job like that!*

After Portugal, we flew to Jersey Island off the coast of France and stayed at a quaint little inn at the bottom of the hill from a castle! Spending two whole weeks with astronauts and inspiring women self-starters got me thinking—*this life is made for me!* I will be forever grateful to my sister and her friends for the incredible adventures that significantly shaped my ideas for what was to come.

Made for more. Somehow, I knew this in my soul even before I returned home to Colorado. I felt like a completely different person than the one who left broken hearted after a brutal breakup. How could I go home as the same girl? Before that trip, I was a girl that just wanted to find love and preferred to stay in her comfort zone over taking any kind of scary risk that could result in failure.

I have worked in retail as a visual merchandising manager for the past several years. I actually like my job, but I must admit that it's beginning to lose its luster after eight years of doing the same thing.

Sometimes the disappointments in life are actually blessings. Before I went to London, I almost missed my flight because I waited around for Mr. Disappointment to change his mind about the breakup. He didn't. So, there I was. Late for an international flight. No agent at the desk to check my bag with. I had quick decisions to make on either giving up or giving it a go and problem solving a way to get on that flight.

Guess what? I did it! I decided to dump the liquids from my suitcase and managed to convince the security people to let me through with no boarding pass. By some miracle, my large, overweight suitcase seamlessly made it through the conveyor belt screening. I held my breath as it barely squeezed through. I was amazed that there was no one there to stop me. The airline gate staff, however, did try to deny me boarding after all the panic, sweat and tears pushed me through what seemed an impossible mission. But after everything else, I even managed to convince them to allow me to board the plane. All of this happened only because of my sheer determination. No matter what, I was going to make it on that flight. And I did. I learned what I was made of that day. I've never looked at a problem the same since. I discovered that there's always a way through. I just have to try, and I will figure it out.

So now what? What is a girl to do when returning home to Colorado after a mind-altering series of two-week adventures in Europe? Throw herself a party of course! And that's exactly what I did. Why not? It was my birthday. It was *his* birthday too. (Queue the deflating balloons and sad violins...) We were supposed to spend our birthday together. It was one of the reasons I didn't want things to end with him. How could a seemingly dream-come-true connection just disappear? I couldn't understand it. But it was time to let go. An epic birthday party seemed appropriate to celebrate my new-found mental freedom. I invited fifteen of my girlfriends. I was astonished that all of them RSVP'd yes. It was a birthday party for the books.

With this new sense of self and what I was capable of, I was determined that I was going to take my life in a new direction. Ideas came in droves from that point. Since I was having all these adventures, then why couldn't I be like all those women I admired and align my ideas with the life that I wanted? Everyday Girl Adventures came alive from this thinking.

To start, I knew I wanted my venture to have a foundation of celebrating moments, big and small. I value my relationships with my daughter, my sisters and my girlfriends. I love spending time doing fun things with the people who matter to me. I also have two adult sons, so don't get me wrong, I do love the special moments I get to spend with them as well. But my mother/daughter Monday dates with my girl, my trips with my sisters, and fun outings with my girlfriends made me realize there is just something special about the bond women naturally share with each other.

It was hard to decide where to begin. But I figured if I was going to start an adventure business the first thing to do was network with inspiring people. I found a group called "Wine, Women and Wealth" on social media. I like wine, I'm a woman, and I want to be wealthy. This seemed like a logical place to start. I decided all these things either applied to me or were where I wanted my life to go. However, going to an event where I didn't know anyone was completely out of my comfort zone. I was terrified. As I walked through the door, I immediately felt that I didn't belong amidst this group of well put-together business women. But to my surprise, they welcomed me with open arms. And that was everything I needed to keep putting myself out there in hopes of making meaningful connections.

I really had no other direction at that point in time. One thing I did know though, is that I like working on a team. My best work in the retail industry has always come through collaboration with others. So, I decided to apply that same thought process with my new venture. From then on, I started putting together events with small business owners. But even though my ideas were starting to take some shape in looking like an actual business, I still felt like a misfit entrepreneur.

In the early days, I attended a lot of networking events to build my contact list and become inspired through others' business journeys. But it was so intimidating to introduce myself to strangers and give them an opportunity to make a judgment call on who I was. People tend to not take me very seriously sometimes. I don't know if it's because I work in retail or if it's simply because I'm a woman that likes to do fun things. I believed it. Having such a low opinion of myself made me think I didn't belong with professional people; "imposter syndrome" is what I'm told this feeling is called. After a few instances of feeling like I was being patronized because I didn't have a "real" business yet, I realized others might view themselves that way too. Embracing another one of my crazy ideas, MissFit Networking was formed–where every "miss" fits.

From that point on, doors of opportunity began to open more and more. I never could have expected that my life was going to go on such a trajectory. So many amazing women have come into my life and joined me on this incredible journey over the course of only seven months. I have jumped at every opportunity available to me. Not only have I made some incredible friends and business partners through this process, but the adventures just keep multiplying. At this current date, I have started a venture called Everyday Girl Adventures event organizing–including 360 slow-motion photo booth services, the MissFit Networking group, and have the Everyday Girl Adventures book in the works. It just goes to show, you never know what you're capable of.

You never know what you can do until you do it.

Although the doubts still creep in, I'm still saying yes to every opportunity. As scary as the unknown is, I am about to embark on the adventure of a lifetime. An actual brick and mortar studio space for my adventure events and a MissFit apparel line and logo that I created! I can't believe I'm actually doing it. I'm starting my own business! Something I never thought I had in me to do. I'm a REAL entrepreneur—even I'm convinced now. I'm going to make my dreams come true. My younger, insecure self, the old me, would be proud of me.

Adventures of a "Miss"chievous Alter-Ego

By Jaime Obertubbesing

You only live once. Cliché? But real. I make most of my decisions on a whim. Not in a wreckless or irresponsible way (well, mostly), but more of "what have I got to lose?". I found that plans often fall through, and I'd rather enjoy the moment than be disappointed. And even though people often think I'm crazy, I have some of the best memories by casting worries (and often, sleep) aside and just going for it! I wish I could say alcohol wasn't a major contribution to many of these adventures, but alas, my good friend, Jack Daniels, and I do have some stories to tell.

I'm drawn to outgoing personalities. My closest friends have always been the ones in the social limelight in one way or another. I've always felt pretty ordinary, and I'm pretty shy until I get comfortable. People are often surprised at the things I've experienced or circles I'm involved in. I'm not the one with great ideas or strong opinions—I often sit in the shadows. I'm adaptable—which I guess is a blessing and a curse. Sometimes I even surprise myself with the adventures I take on. I mean it when I say I'm always up for anything—it matters more to me that I'm enjoying the company I'm with than the activity I'm doing.

My best friend, Kalyn, had moved to Denver that summer. She and her husband snagged a cute studio apartment down the street from the popular hipster hangout, Washington Park—a wealthier, historic, and scenic neighborhood just outside of downtown. A friend and I went up for the weekend and we were excited to see all of what Denver had to offer.

Her husband dropped us off for drinks at Dazzle, a local jazz bar off Lincoln. A friend worked there, and we planned to hit the town at the end of her shift. On the drive, Kalyn's husband told me that he never had to worry when his wife and I were out together, because I was responsible, and he trusted me (I'd known him for several years—somehow I must come across as innocent). I don't know what he was thinking. What I do know is that it all went downhill from there.

A group of friends were at the corner bar down the street so we met up with them there. We ran into a group celebrating their friend who had won the Biggest Loser contest on TV! Naturally, we were intrigued and integrated quite easily into the overwhelming crowd.

The wallflower within me slowly digressed as the drinks went down, and my alter ego, Stacey, appeared. She too, loves Jack Daniels, but can strike up a conversation with anyone around her. Not to mention, her dance moves are impeccable—and, unlike myself, she simply doesn't care if you tell her otherwise. Stacey is everything I wished I could be when I'm sober.

It was she who met Jesse--a 5'9 bachelor in his early 20's, stocky, like a football player. Outgoing, funny, and easy to talk to—we started flirting. I wasn't used to the attention. We spent the next couple of hours talking, like we'd known each other for years. It felt good to not be in the background for once. After several drinks and many laughs on the patio, it was last call and time to switch venues.

Jesse knew the perfect place. His apartment was close by. So, why wouldn't we just continue the party there? We closed out and walked, quite literally, across the street to a fancy looking high-rise. It must have been the alcohol that failed to notice the dim lights in the foyer or how Jesse fumbled with a key to unlock the front door of the entire apartment building. But either way, we were unphased and far too trusting of our new friends. Up the elevator we went to keep the party going.

Jesse warned us that they were renovating. He apologized for the mess of power tools and paint buckets lining the floor of his living room as we tumbled into his domain. Truth be told, we didn't seem to even notice. His friends cracked open some beer and pulled us out the bay window onto the roof overlooking Lincoln Avenue before we had a chance to question. It was breathtaking— something about the expansive view of the city lights and the serene calm at 2am looking down on a ghost town view of one of the busiest streets in downtown Denver. We were literally on the edge, our feet barely touching the end of the overhang from four stories up. It felt so wrong but so free—adrenaline pumping through our 20-something-year-old veins. Jesse kissed me up there, and it was magical. And I felt like I was in a movie—that kind of thing only happens to Stacey, never to me.

But it was not the start of a romance. Something finally clicked across the cold concrete floor on my way to the bathroom. Maybe it was the power cord I tripped over that helped me notice the stacks of tile lining the base of the kitchen island. Or maybe it was the fact that our bar top was actually an oven scattered randomly in the middle of the living room. There was no way anyone lived there, renovation or not. Not even Jesse.

Turns out we'd essentially broken into a newly constructed high-end apartment building that wasn't set to open for a couple more months. Jesse's friends inadvertently ratted him out—he was a contractor working on the units during the day—thus explaining his access. What made him think it'd be a great idea to bring us all there to drink on the roof? Probably the same thing that prompted us to oblige. So the girls and I left abruptly and never heard from Jesse or his friends again.

2 o'clock in the morning is always the best time for fried food, so our mistakes were quickly forgotten as we shifted to frantically finding a place to eat. Fortunately, we were only a mile from the Denver Diner—the classiest joint for a good greasy meal before dawn. My friend was certain she knew exactly how to get there, and took off, practically running, down the street. It took a solid ten minutes to convince her that not only was it a terrible idea to walk so far at this hour of the night, but also that she was headed in the complete opposite direction.

It's unclear how we got back to Kalyn's, but there we were, sitting on the brick wall outside her apartment in the wee hours of the morning, laughing about the events of the evening and our own stupidity. That's when we ran into Tim. Tim lived in the apartments around the corner. Kalyn had met him earlier that week, or so I thought at the time. We ran into him on our way out and decided to see if he wanted to join our outing.

What better to do than go on a walk in the wee hours of the morning? So that's what we did. I mean, we did have Tim with us—so it wasn't like anything bad could happen, right? Well, Tim disappeared. It took a couple of minutes before we realized that he'd stopped to stare into this old, gold Toyota parked along the side of Downing St. Inside was a woman, half disheveled, in her tube top and mini skirt, talking on the phone. Unphased by this in our slightly inebriated state, we continued on our walk to the park, figuring Tim would eventually follow suit.

We were quickly distracted by squeals from the playground. Two girls, about our age, were flying high on the swings, while three guys were propped up against the tree drinking vodka straight from the bottle. Frankly, based on the prior events of the evening, we had no room to judge their decisions, so naturally, we struck up a conversation. The girls were au pairs from France, enjoying a weekend night out on the town, much like ourselves. It's unclear if they knew the guys prior to the park or not. I probably could have told you their whole life story if I hadn't been interrupted by brakes squeaking along the sidewalk. Up pulled the gold Toyota with Tim in the passenger seat. Crazy cell-phone lady was frantically waving at us to jump in. What inspired us to get inside that car? Clearly not good intuition.

Let's call her Izabell—the tall, mysterious, woman that just picked up three wandering drunks in the middle of the night. She was twice our age and had a thick accent I couldn't quite pin down. By some miracle, the car quickly came to a halt outside a skyrise apartment building. As if we'd known this woman for years, we followed her down the winding hallways on the way to her 3rd floor apartment. For what? It still wasn't clear. Well, Tim sure found his agenda, when Izabell stripped off her top and casually flashed her fake boobs in the elevator. But yet, somehow we were still invested.

Her apartment was artsy and retro, with bright colors and patterns covering the walls. Izabell reached for an ice bucket full of shooters, as if she'd been awaiting our arrival all night, and abruptly suggested we go swimming. Despite the fact that none of us keep swim suits on hand for such spontaneous swimming occasions, we decided that seemed like a fabulous idea. It was an outdoor pool in the middle of her urban apartment complex. Did this stop us? Of course not. There had to be someone that popped out and got a free show from their balcony that night.

The heated pool was not so hot, so our polar plunge was short-lived. Unfortunately, towels were also an afterthought. The sauna was the next best option. I never thought I'd have such in-depth conversations, topless in a sauna with strangers. But there we were, wearing our hearts on our sleeves in the dead of the night. One thing's for certain—Tim sure must have been having the time of his life.

Eventually sunlight peeked through the alleys of the apartment complex, signaling time to go. Turns out, we'd never even made it out of the neighborhood—just two blocks away from home.

13 years later, I am still often the wallflower. I still sit in the shadows of my friends. I still hate making decisions, and I still don't have strong opinions in most situations. But what I don't need is Stacey to have an adventure. Similar scenarios (though slightly more responsible ones) that would have taken multiple drinks to initiate are things I will now

do sober. I have learned that memories are more important, and I'd rather live for the moment than hold back, because life is too short to regret missing out on an opportunity to look back on and smile.

"Miss"led Adventures of Becoming a Mom

By Tiffany McKee

My kids are feral. I'd rather have wild raccoons come into my house than have my kids ask for dinner.

Maddox is ten, but as big as a 14-year-old. Lilah is turning 15 in July.

I thought motherhood would be scarier–that I wouldn't be a good mom. Growing up without a mother myself, I thought I wasn't ready. In fact, I never thought I wanted any kids, out of fear I wouldn't make the cut–like my own mother couldn't, apparently. From her example alone, I thought it would be too hard and that I'd give up. But, I ended up with a surprise–I was becoming a mom regardless.

And as scared as I was, in that moment, I knew I had to change my mindset. I suddenly *knew* I could do it and give her, and any future child I had, the best life. I *would* be better than my mother. I owed it to this little baby I was growing.

I envisioned pregnancy to be rainbows and unicorns. I never thought I'd be sick all the time. I never thought I'd be high risk with both. And I never thought I'd fear losing any pregnancies in between. But I did. Even these negative experiences shaped me to push forward for my kids even more after they were born. My life would never be as great as it is if I hadn't gotten pregnant.

I absolutely hated being pregnant. It's hot and sweaty, not to mention the diet restrictions. I couldn't even eat cheddar cheese! I nearly died with both, actually. With Lilah, I had preeclampsia starting at 29 weeks–they hospitalized me until my kidneys started to fail at 34 weeks and I had a crash emergency C-section. She was 4lbs 5oz. The next day she lost weight and was only 3lb 15oz. Surprisingly, she only spent 13 days in the NICU.

I suffered two miscarriages after her. One at 12 weeks, one at 20. We tried to conceive for four years! Maddox was my rainbow baby. I carried him until 37 weeks and had a successful VBAC (vaginal birth after C-section), but 38 hours of labor and four failed epidurals, so I felt EVERYTHING.

Hence why two has always been enough for me. After pregnancy and the bond of breastfeeding was my favorite, though. Sometimes I think of my heavenly babies.

What surprised me most is I was never as emotionally or physically tired in the subsequent months after birth as all other mothers described. I am already a highly energetic person to begin with—but regardless, the physical and emotional taxation that having a child should take on a person—I never had or felt that in the slightest. I jumped out of bed excited to change them, excited to feed them again—excited to try new foods. And for that, I'm grateful. In fact, having an infant or toddler or non-school-aged child was way less tiresome for me than it is now.

Now, it's never seeing them between work and school. Days are incredibly long—

from 4am until 10pm, getting myself ready for work, the kids packed up for a long day at school, and everything squeezed in before bed. It's so much more incredibly hard now. And sometimes I wish I could go back to those moments where I could stay in my pajamas a little longer and put on a sensory show while they're in a high chair throwing all of their food on the floor instead of eating it (The sensory show is for me, by the way). I miss those days, to be quite honest. Now it's time to come up with the money for a car for Delilah next year and then start saving for her college in the next three. Motherhood is sometimes the best and worst 'hood' I've ever lived in.

Anyone under the age of 15 is gross in general. Where do I start...nail biting, leaving poop in the toilet, mayo on corn dogs. I found a half-eaten sandwich in one of Maddox's hats. I can only hope for cleaner days!

I never thought I'd have to say:

"Stop smearing poop into the carpet."

"My name isn't bruh."

"Maddox, don't tell anyone about your sister's fart corner."

"You can't call people hillbillies to their faces."

"Stop telling your cousin he's adopted."

"No, you can't have the CVV to my credit card."

All true stories, and now I'm laughing in bed. Especially about Maddox telling my nephew he's adopted in public. Why is this my life?

Some days my favorite thing is just going to bed–being a mother is exhausting. But when I see them sleeping soundly, I know I'm doing all the right things. And they're really funny, so I always have entertainment!

I'll write the rest when these feral raccoons go to sleep. Speaking of being a mom.

Can we include all of my bad luck in this story? I currently have someone coming to fix the heating coil in my fridge, the heating unit in my dryer, and Lilah just broke the door to my dishwasher. Nevertheless, I'm still smiling.

My life is chaos, hence me thriving in it–I've been given no choice. Like being waterboarded every single day. One time Lilah jumped off the side of the pontoon (life jacket on) while I wasn't looking, into Lake Pueblo– the dirtiest water on the planet. I had to jump in after her. My soul left my body. She was six. At three years old, Maddox dragged his little Mater powered car up the stairs and said, "Mommy, look at me!", sitting in it, about to go down those eleven stairs. I didn't know I could make it up there in two strides with my tiny legs! That could've ended very badly.

They are brave, fearless, and surprisingly have had zero broken bones to date. Is it by the grace of God? Or just really, *really* good luck? I'll never know. But thank goodness for life jackets and hyper-aware moms.

Fears. I fear everything with my kids. Now my daughter is about to drive. Every time I see a car crash, I get major anxiety. If I hear about something bad happening to a child, my brain wanders. Will someone break their heart (or their legs)? Are they getting bullied? I'm working on that, they need *freedom*–I just want to protect them from everything bad.

Nearly 15 years of mom memories…too many to count, and it's really hard to choose my favorites. But one of the best was probably living in Hawaii. Lilah was young and amazed by everything (but scared of the sea turtles)–the beaches, the culture, the food you cannot get anywhere else–she LOVED it! And so did I. We never wanted to leave. It's also where I got pregnant with Maddox after my lost pregnancies and trying for another for so long. It's where another adventure began, completing my circle.

My favorite memory…my wedding. It was so special to have Maddox walk me down the pathway and give me away. The pride on his face. And the way he *cried* the whole ceremony. And Delilah was the most beautiful maid of honor ever. It was like, in that moment, they were proud of *me* instead of the other way around!

Every single aspect of parenting so far has been an obstacle. But the challenges have brought so many rewards! From pregnancy losses and hard births, to being a 10-year military spouse, and then suddenly becoming a single parent in a matter of 15 years. But it's those little moments–my daughter hugging me out of nowhere; my son asking me to watch him play a game. Or getting excited they passed a hard test. I'd face every single obstacle over and over again for them.

To be honest, I wish someone had told me how much your feelings would be hurt the first time your child "resents" you for something. Co-parenting is not for the weak. I wish someone had described how to navigate explaining death to them too. We've lost quite a few people the last two years and...it's a helpless feeling when you're supposed to have the answers. Moms always do, right?

What would I do differently? Honestly, nothing. I can't even pick one thing I'd change other than leave my ex sooner. But, even *that* set me up for success. I would've never met my husband and all four of us wouldn't have what we do now with each other. The kids wouldn't have Bobby in their lives if I had left my previous marriage sooner than it ended.

The best advice I can give is to forgive yourself ahead of time. You're going to screw up, you're going to be a crappy parent at times, you're going to FAIL them. So do yourself the favor beforehand, know those things, accept them and those moments will come and pass easier.

I'm most proud of making it through the fires of being a below-poverty-line, single mother of two after my divorce. I'm most proud of always making it work for Delilah and Maddox even if it meant I went without. I'm most proud of being an amazing mother.

Adventures of a "Miss"tical Traveler

By Romina Cela

We all have that one moment in life—that moment when your world suddenly stops. When the lens with which you see things shifts, the focus changes, and the picture is finally clear as day. This moment happens at different stages in life. For me, it happened standing on top of a hill, overlooking a lush, green expanse. My breathing and my movements slowed down. Everything around me quieted. My eyes narrowed, as if to take in every single speckle of dust in the air. My thoughts came to a halt. And in that moment, I felt a sense of belonging, of understanding my place, of knowing where I could be and think, and just forget that the world existed—Scotland.

I had traveled to plenty of places and countries across Europe and the U.S., but always with friends. It was June of 2012 when I would embark on my first "solo" travel as an adult. I left behind my family and kids to attend a week-long class in Scotland, studying Scottish literature and history. However, preparation started before the class itself. We were supposed to familiarize ourselves with the material we were going to study. Reading Burns every night became an exciting routine. Trying to pronounce his words became a joyful event as I stumbled on each word attempting to give justice to the Scottish accent. But with each passing day, I was feeling more accomplished on my pronunciation and ready to undertake my new adventure.

My flight from Germany was fairly short and uneventful. Instructions were provided for us to navigate the train and bus system in order to get to our final destination of Saint Andrews. I zoomed through the Edinburgh airport to find my way to the train station. I think I had a smile plastered on my face just from listening to the thick Scottish accents that surrounded me. I found myself concentrating hard to make sure I correctly understood everything that was being spoken to me when I had to stop and ask for directions. However, I had a sense of joy and happiness I only felt when I was in Scotland. I think I would have been blissfully happy even if I had found myself lost.

At last, I managed to get to our temporary residency in Saint Andrews: Rockview, a typical gray, stone, stoic looking villa overlooking the water and surrounded by the famous Saint Andrews Golf Course. It seemed like the type of place filled with history, like it had been there for centuries. High ceilings and long, thick curtains were just some of things that got my attention at first glance. The view outside the panel windows was breathtaking. The water splashing furiously on the rocky shore gave a glimpse of how cold the winters might be there, while you would be sitting cozy and warm, feeling protected from the elements inside this glorious house. I started walking from room to room and made a full stop in the sitting room. I was enthralled by the massive library taking up two full wall panels—it looked like something out of a movie. Thoughts kept going through my mind, wondering how old these books might be. *Had the inhabitants of the house read them all?* I thought of the hands that touched them—the stories they told. I closed my eyes and just stood there, smelling the room, wanting to be a page in one of those books. Ann, the owner of the house, was pleasant enough to let me peruse and even go through some of them. I found a corner in the house overlooking the water, where I would sit and read every day, losing myself completely to another time, another place, or another story from the great storytellers of Scotland, such as Robert Burns and Sir Walter Scott.

During our week-long stay we toured Edinburgh, Stirling Castle, Lochleven Castle (a tiny piece of island where Mary Queen of Scotts was exiled to), various abbeys, famous bookstores, and cathedrals. Every place I stepped, I stepped on history. I walked in someone else's footsteps. I kept wondering and picturing Scotland during its dark and bloodied war with England—the neurons in my brain scrambling to keep up with all the new information that I was eagerly absorbing. I felt insatiable. I wanted to learn more, to see more. I felt paralyzed with fear that the day to leave was quickly and quietly approaching.

I went on whiskey tours that left me feeling like a dragon with its nose smoking.

Note to self: stay away from whiskey with any level of smokiness in it. I got called out by guards at the Edinburgh castle to climb down from the rocks from which I was graciously posing. I felt an unknown presence and bone chilling temperature in an empty abbey room (and yes, I did run out!). The one thing I was unable to bring myself to do was try Haggis, an experience I braved during another visit when I went back with my friend, Jean. If you don't know what that is, I dare you to look it up. It was banned from the U.S. in 1971, if that gives you any idea just how terrible it is. Needless to say, each day was filled to the brim with events tailored to culture and history submersion. However, it was the last day that left an indelible print.

We had one more place to visit–a place called Scott's View, so named after its most frequent visitor, Sir Walter Scott. The place was far from our dwellings in St. Andrews, so we were transported by a minibus. I remember looking outside the window and taking in the beautiful landscape and droves of cattle. The ride was close to an hour long. We finally arrived at our destination and were happy to just roam around and stretch our legs. We felt like a bunch of loud and obnoxious kindergarten kids left out to run amok. I moved around the vehicle to take in the view, and that's when my world came to a screeching halt. The noise around me dissipated. I could hear my own heartbeat. I could hear my thoughts. I felt like I had found my axis. I gazed at the expanse of hills in front of me, shades of green going on endlessly. Nothing and no one seemed to matter. Everything around me disappeared. I felt a magnetic pull like nothing I had ever felt before. I felt like I was home–I had found my place. I was no longer lost. Moisture filled my eyes and I realized I was overwhelmed with emotion, so much so that I started to cry. Tears of joy, fulfillment, and realization. I sat on that bench, took a deep breath, and wiped my quiet tears away. At thirty-two years old I had found my happy place. A place that I would later find myself being drawn to, missing, and always longing to revisit. In Robert Burns' words, "But to see her was to love her, love but her and her forever". While Burn's poem was about a girl, for me it rang so true about my love for Scotland.

I would find myself crying again in Scotland, but this time it was because I was leaving, afraid to part with that feeling of wholesomeness. Looking back on it now, I should have known better. I never truly left Scotland. And while I've been back to visit regularly still, I know a chunk of my heart is still there waiting for me to join the pieces together, permanently.

Adventures of a "Miss"hap-hazard Sourdough Baker

By Kam Fletcher

I don't know about you, but I love bread! I've enjoyed baking since my gran would make biscuits with me whenever I went to visit her.

When I first got married, 41 years ago, my husband, Andy, and I moved to Switzerland. Interestingly enough, he was going to go and teach at his former high school, while I was going back to my family's birthplace. Loving food as I do, I wanted to discover my country's dishes, which were simple and made with local ingredients. On top of that, the bread was the best bread I've ever tasted. We lived in Switzerland twice. The first time in Zurich; the second time in Geneva—the

French part of Switzerland where our daughter, Maren, and son, Dylan, went to Swiss-French schools. Lots of baking and chocolate eating happened in their schools. In 4th grade, they even learned how to make wine!

It wasn't till we left Switzerland and moved to Colorado that I started baking bread seriously. This is where Dylan, my son, comes in. He spent seven and a half years in Switzerland and, I feel, was greatly influenced by the simple good food and bread. He wasn't interested in cooking while living in Colorado, yet I should have seen some creative talent when he was asked to make a quiche Lorraine for his French class in high school. He was given the recipe, and since he hadn't cooked much before, I helped a bit. The amazing thing was he decorated the pie crust without any help and it looked like a professional had done it. This was before YouTube or Pinterest existed to show you how. In college, Dylan majored in art, and they do say artists make great chefs.

After college Dylan became a chef in Montana. He learned the basics as a cook in numerous restaurants. He later moved to Portland where he was a sous chef in a few places. He also worked for two different bakeries—one owned by Ken Forkish who taught him how to make sourdough bread. Ken's books, bakery, and other restaurants have won numerous James Beard awards. Dylan got a great start.

Where am I in all this? I wanted to learn how to make sourdough. This was seven and a half years ago, and with the help of Dylan, who taught me everything he knew (and still does), I began my journey. I also learned a lot from Chuck Robinove, a bread baker, tester, and writer in Colorado Springs. Well, Chuck had worked with another famous sourdough baker, Peter Reinhardt. How fortunate was I?

If you knew me when I started out, you were very lucky. I would give everyone my bread: pita bread, herb breads, rolls, cinnamon bread, pizza dough, chocolate chip cookies, naan, soft pretzels—you name it, because you can make sourdough anything. My friends also wanted some of my sourdough starter, which I gladly shared.

In the sourdough community, everyone names their starter. It's just like a pet–you have to feed the starter, or it will die. My starters were special because I had one named Emily and another named Ken, in honor of the man who taught us the craft. Well, I went to Iowa to my grandson, Ole's, first birthday party and wanted to make sourdough pretzels, which he loves. He lives ten hours away and so I had to bring Ken with me to make the pretzels. Oops— I used up all the starter for the pretzels. Ken died. No worries, Emily was waiting at home. I simply fed her a few times and my new second starter was born. His name, of course, was Ole.

For two years, my friends wanted me to sell my bread. To be honest, I didn't have the confidence. I was making so many mistakes. I also felt it would take too much time in my little kitchen and not be profitable. I'm a people person who is very community-minded and has spent most of my life working or teaching kids and adults. I couldn't imagine being in an industrial kitchen by myself baking bread.

COVID-19 came and my husband's work as a lecturer in international schools around the world dried up. At first, since we are old, we were too nervous to teach, because we were at risk for COVID. Andy thought he could teach around the world on Zoom. That didn't work, because the students were all "zoomed out". I took a long-term sub reading specialist job, which led me to being a part-time reading teacher now. But three days a week wasn't enough.

I finally decided it was time to start teaching adults and children how to make easy sourdough bread on their time schedule. I had all these ideas for why this could be a worthwhile venture. For one thing, you don't have to be an accomplished baker or even cook to make sourdough bread. Not to mention, it is so much healthier than the store bought bread that has twenty ingredients in it.

In fact, the health benefits are numerous. Due to long fermentation of the sourdough dough, the gluten is broken down, making the bread more digestible. This helps people with gluten intolerance–I found that many of my friends with gluten issues could eat my bread. There are also probiotics in sourdough bread that make it a better choice than the commercially processed bread at the store. Probiotics help to support the gut microbiome by producing gut bacteria that aid the body in healthy digestion. If you are worried about blood sugar, bread can actually be part of a balanced meal if you add healthy fats and proteins. With the importance of community in my life and wishing to help people live healthier lives, I thought to myself, teaching sourdough bread might just be the ticket to help both our family and people in the Colorado Springs community.

But all the mistakes? You know what, no matter what mistakes I made, the bread kept turning out. So that's how I got my name–the Haphazard Sourdough Baker. One story of my haphazardness was when I was making the dough for my cinnamon twists. On a little notecard, I had the recipe for one batch on the left side and two batches on the right. You know what's coming: I started the dry ingredients looking at the single batch side. Then, in my style, I followed the double batch recipe for the liquid ingredients. Most people would have done the math and just added the extra dry ingredients. Me? No. I started throwing in flour like I was Lucille Ball in *I love Lucy* during her chocolate candy factory scene. She was throwing chocolate pieces all over the conveyor belt with chocolate flying everywhere. I was throwing flour all over—very dramatically mind you—trying to get the right proportions. I finally gave up and took the dough home. But I didn't throw it away. Instead, I baked it, and (drum roll please) it still turned out!

I've been teaching people of all ages from 3 to 92 years-old for a year now, with the goal of sharing my knowledge of sourdough, building community, having fun, and making (hopefully) some dough! I have done date-night classes, family classes, mother-daughter and sons' night out, bridal showers, friend's classes—you name it. I also do children's birthday parties where they make their own pizza, pop tarts, or cinnamon twists.

Community is very important to me, and I wanted to build that in my business. Well, I feel it happened. After Thanksgiving, our dishwasher broke and flooded the main floor. I had to cancel two classes. Soon after, I posted photos of the torn-up kitchen. Amazingly, six families who I had taught to make sourdough bread—during the holiday season mind you—offered their kitchens to me for classes or whatever I needed. I was so touched and thankful for my sourdough community.

I am very grateful to have formed the Haphazard Sourdough Baker Company surrounded by such a supportive community. Thanks for hanging in there and listening to my story.

Adventures of a "Miss"calculated Girls Night Out

by Sheridan West

Have you ever had a time in your life where you wish that you could just redo it all? If the answer is yes, then you've come to just the right place. Allow me a chance to tell you my story.

It was finally time to see one of my favorite bands, The Neighbourhood, in Denver! I was so excited! My sister and I arrived at the Ogden, located on Colfax Avenue. For those of you who don't know, Colfax Avenue is not the safest street in the area to be around late at night. It was extremely difficult to find free parking. After driving past several expensive lots, I finally found a free, restaurant parking lot next to the venue. Hooray! I struck gold!

My sister, ever so graciously, pointed to a sign on the fence that said, "Restaurant parking only. Violators will be towed." However, I checked online and the restaurant closed at midnight. I knew that the concert would end before then and personally didn't think that the restaurant employees would even be able to keep track of who violated the rule. I convinced us both that it was all going to be fine. We parked there and walked across the street to the venue.

The concert was phenomenal. After it ended, we walked back to the car. To our surprise, it was nowhere to be found! Instant panic mode set in—I honestly thought that it was stolen! I began searching the parking lot until I noticed those lovely tow truck signs that my sister pointed out earlier in the evening. It finally hit me—my car had been towed! I shared my newfound discovery with my sister as she gritted her teeth and tried her best not to say those infamous words you hear when you don't follow wise instructions: "I told you so!"

To make matters worse, my phone battery was only at 20 percent. I couldn't help but to still be in denial as I called the number on the sign. A nice lady answered. I instantly explained that I wasn't sure where my car went. I then proceed to ask the dreaded question, "Was my car towed to your company?". She then responded with a giggle, "I really hope it wasn't, but I'd be happy to check our systems to be sure. Can I get the make, model and color of the vehicle?" I provided her with the details and suddenly heard the daunting sound of typing on a computer keyboard. I don't know about you, but hearing that sound as I was desperately waiting for a response just made me more anxious! My fingers started sweating, my knees instantly got weak, and my stomach was knotting up. I couldn't help but feel like the entire world was about to flip upside down. Finally, she responded, "Yes! We received your car this evening at 10:30 pm from a restaurant parking lot off of Colfax Avenue." My heart instantly sank. As grateful as I was that my car wasn't stolen, I still couldn't believe that this was happening! I asked where the tow truck company was located and plugged in the address. It was only a thirteen minute drive! "Great, let's catch a ride and get your car!" my sister said, as she sighed in relief.

Now, in 2015, I was super skeptical of ride-sharing apps. Between all of the news stories I had seen and personally knowing someone who had a negative experience with one, I did not want to put us at risk. Therefore, a cab was the best solution to arrive at our destination quickly and safely. As we stood in the empty parking lot, I began searching for cab companies in the area and called every single one on the list. I received several busy signals. We suddenly came up with an idea to brainstorm a list of every friend who lived in the area. Unfortunately, I only had the number for one friend. Last time I checked her social media, she was in Mexico.

"Where could we go?", "Who could we call?", and "What were we to do?" are the questions that I frantically asked myself as I watched the light at the end of the tunnel become dimmer. We agreed that the only reasonable idea was to start walking there and continue calling around for a pickup. I pulled up my GPS and converted the drive time to walking distance. The GPS stated 3.9 miles which equated to 1 hour 21 minutes. I figured that we could use the GPS to navigate and we could memorize steps along the way to conserve battery. In case you didn't know, GPS stands for "God's Positioning System", and you'll see why soon enough.

As we walked, we had a trifecta of strange encounters. First, this black SUV kept circling the block we were walking on. After the third time, the vehicle stopped near us and the tinted windows rolled down. "Hey beautiful ladies. Where are you headed?" a man's voice questioned from the inside. We noticed that this vehicle was full of men who did not look like they had the best intentions. As tempting as it was, I could not in good conscience ask them for a ride to the tow truck company, so we ignored them and continued walking. We heard a closing statement, "Wow! It's like that? Have a good night then." The window rolled up and the SUV sped off. Phew! We dodged the first strange encounter.

50 minutes into our walking journey, we faced the second strange encounter. A homeless man across the street was yelling at us, "Hey! You two should come over here and hang out with me!" All we could do was increase our walking speed and watch our backs! We didn't want any trouble, and this was getting ridiculous! Still no answers from the cab companies or friends. I decided that I didn't want to waste any more of my dwindling battery power attempting to track down someone. But there was one thing I knew for sure; I was NOT calling my parents. I did not want to be read the riot act for asking them to drive over an hour out of town in the middle of the night to pick us up. 31 more minutes of walking is all we had left! Even though our feet were killing us, we mustered up the strength to finish the journey.

As we got closer, I realized that my phone battery was on the verge of death. The GPS was giving inaccurate directions, so I called the tow truck company one last time and asked for verbal walking directions. My sister and I worked together to memorize them. The employee advised us that her shift was over at 3:00am and if we didn't get there by then, we would have to wait until the next employee arrived later that morning before getting my vehicle. I checked the time and it was officially closer to 2:00am. The pressure was on, and time was of the essence! I shut off my phone to conserve the drop of battery remaining in case an emergency came up. We were officially exhausted and growing wearier with each remaining step, but we kept the momentum going.

Finally, the tow truck company sign beamed in the distance! We were only five minutes away from the promised land! We had just begun celebrating when the final encounter of the trifecta happened. Suddenly, we heard barking. I didn't think anything of it. But my sister screamed "RUUNNNNN!" without any explanation and took off running. She used to run track, so she darted off quickly into a nearby ditch next to a train track and left me behind! I turned to the right and saw two Pitbulls barking and running directly towards me! I wish I would've known Pitbull Rule Number One beforehand: *if a Pitbull charges at you, resist the impulse to scream and run away. Remain motionless, hands at your sides, and avoid eye contact.* Well, it's not every day that one encounters Pitbull charges! So instead I took off running in response to fear and followed my sister into the nearby ditch to avoid the dogs. Those dogs must've been really motivated because they found a way into the ditch and continued chasing me! I thought that I could outrun them, but the dogs were inching closer and closer. My sister had jumped out of the ditch and was so far ahead. I saw her turn around, grab rocks, and start heading my way to try to protect me. I was running out of breath and decided to just let the dogs attack and eat me alive.

Remember "God's Positioning System"? Yes, this was that moment–the moment where I saw my life flash before my eyes and knew that I was going to have to fight for my life. Then, out of nowhere, I heard the sound of a train's air horn honking repeatedly. I could vaguely see the conductor, but I have no doubt in my mind that it was an angel from Heaven above conducting that train at two in the morning. I suddenly heard the dogs squealing behind me. I turned my head around quickl,y and I saw the pitbulls stop, turn around and start running the opposite direction! I was in complete shock when I realized that I could stop running. I was sweating and exasperated. The only reaction I could even think of was to burst into tears and fall to the ground. My sister ran over to me with rocks still in her hands, dropping them once she saw that I was fine. She comforted me and reminded me to breathe. Once I collected myself, I looked slightly upward and saw the promised land. My sister said, "Everything is going to be ok. We made it in time." She helped me up, and we walked to the building.

At the window, I heard that friendly voice say, "Are you ok? I thought you weren't going to make it in time." I was still recovering my breath with sweat dripping down my face, but I managed to say, "We just walked over an hour to get here, got chased by dogs, and at this point, I'm ready to be home now." She gave me a look of shock and she said, "Well don't worry, darling. I'll get you taken care of. It'll be $275.05". At that point, I couldn't even react to how expensive that amount was. All I wanted was to be sitting in my car with the A/C blasting and driving home. I gave her my debit card, and she guided us to my car. My sister and I got in, and I just cried again as she comforted me. We still had an hour and 15 minute drive home. Of course, our parents were worried sick, and once we got home, they read me the riot act anyway! Darn, I thought I'd get a pass after the disaster I just lived. Guess we all can't get what we wish for!

Do I regret that the events of this night ever happened? Sometimes, yes! However, I've come to realize that life is our greatest teacher and that the lessons we learn can help others navigate their life's journeys. Several years later, I even had a chance to pay it forward and help two college girls who found themselves in the same situation that my sister and I had. Henry Ford said it best, and I quote, "Failure is the opportunity to begin again, only this time more wisely." I challenge you today to avoid always looking for the large, red 'redo' button that we all tend to search for as we're enduring life's difficulties, but instead to find the silver linings.

The Italian Adventures of a "Miss"guided Tourist

By Kay Rowe

Due to popular demand, I documented my trip to Italy in 2015, including research that preceded the trip. I hope you find this useful if/when you travel there and that you have a laugh or two in the process.

I first posted my Italian vacation as an event on my meet-up group pages in early February. I was seeking recommendations on the best time of year, prices, where to visit, and in general, how to "do" the trip. I met with a travel agent and checked out package offers, but I finally concluded that it was more cost effective to plan the trip myself without all the bells and whistles. Besides, we were up for an adventure and preferred serendipity, so who needs a tour guide?

After talking to many Italians directly, I chose Northern Italy and the Tuscany region for my visit. It helped that the Milan airport, Malpensa, had the lowest airfares of the major International Airports in Italy. The month of April was deemed best for economical purposes, and the weather looked great too—the average temperatures tend to range from low 50's to mid 70's with minimal rain during that time.

Packing light is wise considering you have to drag your luggage around with you. I took the regulation size carry-ons and even those turned out to be too much for two weeks. No kidding–I could have cut it down by half.

Renting a vehicle proved much better for flexibility and being able to go places not easily accessed by rail. However, next time I'd like to do a combination of the two, staying overnight in various locations for two to three nights and taking day trips by rail. That would markedly cut down on the driving and, more importantly, the stress on the driver. **Needless to say,** we had some heated "back seat driver" moments. As I recall, each one of us had a turn taking a walk to cool off. My walk was the longest. When I couldn't find my friends after a couple of hours of trying to find someone who spoke English, the thought crossed my mind that they may have actually ditched me! What a relief when I finally saw the car turn the corner.

The roads up to villages are very tiny, lucky if two small cars can fit through at the same time. So, if you rent a vehicle, a small one may be best. However, considering they only come with manual transmissions, we ignored our own advice and ended up with a less-than-tiny SUV. The protocol is to politely back up to let the other driver pass when you have a tight squeeze—very interesting when you are on a windy road up in the mountains! Oh, and you may want to avoid tunnels. If we hadn't pulled the mirrors in, we would have had some "splainin'" to do upon returning the rental.

To find your way, adjusting the GPS settings to an Italian accent is absolutely necessary. But despite the attractive intonation, the GPS is truly only as efficient as the data entered into it. Therefore, a good old paper map may have been the way to go. Sometimes we would reach our "destination", only to find it was in fact, not the destination, but a sign leading to more signs to follow. We often had to ask locals for assistance. Thank goodness they were friendly beyond belief, and if they didn't speak English, they'd go out of their way to find someone who did. Some of the wait staff even tried to help us speak Italian—needless to say, I learned how to properly say "Grazie!" ("thank you") very quickly.

Heavily toured areas such as Venice, Florence, and Pisa had a lot of foreign vendors selling items that were not actually made in Italy. I made a point of checking the labels to be sure I was getting Italian-made items instead of Chinese and Indian imports. Also be warned that there are pick pockets everywhere—so keep your funds secure. I even recommend using special wallets that prevent credit card numbers from being swiped.

The food and wine–absolutely amazing, no matter what the venue. I prefer gluten-free but found that I could consume Italian wheat with no issues. Not to mention, the raviolis are thinner, with more filling and less pasta, and the pizzas are more like flat-breads. Amaretti cookies (also known as Italian macaroons) are made with almond meal and risotto with rice flour. And the dining experience was also quite surprising. We found it interesting that when given the option of standing or sitting, there was a surcharge for choosing the latter. Bars would include free charcuterie-type appetizers with a glass of wine. And most accommodations included breakfast and even allowed us to fill take-out containers for picnics we could have along the way to our next destination! I could get used to that kind of service! Needless to say, we didn't have to spend much on food.

Now that you have all the advice, I should get on with my adventure.

Our journey began on April 15 on a flight from Newark to Malpensa. Upon arrival, Deb, Nancy, and I acquired the aforementioned gargantuan rental car and set off on our Italian adventure. After a quick stop at La Pastacceria for pastries, we headed towards our first destination—a bed and breakfast in Brunate, near Lake Como, at the B&B Al Parco Marenghi at Via Mulattiera per San Maurizio 24/Angolo Via Scalini Brunate, 22034, Italy (in case you wanted to the exact coordinates). Italian addresses are something else! I had received an email from the property owner explaining that the lodge was "up a hill", which I took to mean "a steep incline". However, as we drove and drove... *and drove* (for 45 minutes), we soon discovered that "up a hill" more closely translated to "top of a mountain". Fortunately, the owner redeemed himself as he proved quite helpful in mapping out our upcoming route to Venice.

We traveled by way of the southern side of the Italian Alps to Sondria, making many stops along the way. Every village was unique—the first was at the ski lifts. Heading to another, we spotted a strange, large building in the distance that resembled stacked shipping containers. As we got closer, we realized it was, in fact, just stacked shipping containers. Other villages were very quaint with narrow streets and passageways, all intricately weaving in and around buildings with long, narrow stairways. And nearly everyone has a cat guarding the doorway.

Things were going well until we got to Bolzano on Saturday. Perhaps the American-accented GPS would have served us better, because instead of directing us to our lodge, we found ourselves at a directional sign marked "20 kilometers". We were lost. Fortunately, a resident saw us stopped and struggling with directions. Although she didn't speak much English, she offered to help saying "Americana? Me no speak English. I get brother. He speak English". I wasn't exaggerating when I said Italian's really go out of their way to help, because she walked all the way home to fetch him and half an hour later he arrived to assist with directions. We stopped to eat at Babsi and called our accommodations to let them know our situation. The owner's mother took the call, confirming our room was still available. However, much to our surprise, during our meal, the owner showed up in person to let us know there was a mistake and our room was actually taken. In the midst of her apologizing, I noticed a section on the menu advertising rooms for rent on premises. 75 Euros a night for all three of us. So, in true serendipitous fashion, we stayed at one of their apartments instead.

After our tour of Venice we stayed in Noale, at Hotel Due Torri Tempesta. You may be wondering, "Why didn't they stay in Venice?" The answer: very crowded and expensive. We were also concerned about the weather forecast predicting heavy rain and possible flooding. If you didn't know, Venice is built on a group of 118 small islands that are separated by canals and linked by over 400 bridges. The city also has a reputation for pick pocketing, so we opted to lodge elsewhere.

We drove onto and through Bologna and Florence before staying in Livergnone at a horse training farm called Red Rose Ranch. This is literally where prize-winning race horses are trained. I had the pleasure of meeting one of their buddies: a donkey. This is a short story all in itself: I was taking a walk past multiple corrals and heard something that seemed to be following behind me. I no sooner turned around and looked over my right shoulder. My eyes were met with donkey's and he let out a very loud "hee-haw", baring his teeth. Of course, I made good use of the opportunity and took several selfies. That evening we had dinner in Leoni. There were so many delicious items to choose from that we created our very own private buffet, selecting our favorites and sharing. We had starters, main dishes, dessert and, of course, wine.

By Wednesday we were en route to Florence, but not through the city. There was a park where tourists could view the city from a distance, and we stayed a while and took a lot of photos. Our next stop was a café where we met Ray Fox, an architect from San Diego. Ray happened to overhear us talking about driving all the way to Cortona (where *Under the Tuscan Sun* was filmed) in hopes of attending a cooking class that we were not even able to confirm. He told us about his friends who owned a business that not only had a cooking class, but a restaurant, vineyard, winery and lodging as well. So on to Chianti Country we went instead, to stay at Fattoria Montagliari in Greve.

Once again, we were met with a directional sign, "20 Kilometers", but, learning from our previous experience, continued on to eventually arrive at what we thought was a portion of the property. No one was there, so we assumed it was not open yet. We spotted a gazebo where we made ourselves comfortable with some leftovers from the previous BNB and, of course, a bottle of wine. Much to our surprise, three women showed up on horseback. We explained that we were waiting for the place to open and hoped no one would mind that we were hanging out enjoying a glass of wine. One of the women spoke out (in perfect English with an Italian accent), "You are at the wrong place." My friend Deb, with as straight a face as she could muster, asked, "What do you think the owner will do if they find us here?" The woman's reply, with an equally straight face: "They'll probably kill you."

Fortunately, she wasn't serious, but to be on the safe side we didn't chance a meeting with the owners. And wouldn't you know it? Another 20 kilometers in the opposite direction, and we arrived at our actual destination.

We were famished, so we checked into lodging as quickly as possible then headed down to dinner. It was so beautiful outdoors and we got seated on the patio where we were greeted by a special guest (the resident cat) who had been following us from the moment we arrived. The cat was well-mannered so our dinner was not interrupted too dramatically. He just weaved in and out and around our legs and made minor attempts to jump on our laps.

The next morning we took our cooking class, which was absolutely amazing. We made cauliflower steaks, grilled with a mixture of olive oil and garlic, served on a thin slice of Italian bread. We then made pasta egg noodles from scratch and boiled them to perfection once they were ready to go. The meat sauce was also made from scratch with plenty of garlic, Italian herbs, tomatoes and ground veal. Dessert was Zagliatone, an Italian dessert (also considered a beverage) made with egg yolks, sugar, and a sweet wine (usually Moscato d'Asti or Marsala). There were at least three bottles of wine, each one paired with the appropriate dish. After a full day in the kitchen, cooking and consuming the fruits of our labor, we were given a tour of the winery. They provided us with plenty of left-overs, including more wine (we were definitely happy about that!). Then we were on our way to Montecatini AltoTerme, a medieval village, to stay at Casa Gala.

Saturday we went on through Lucca, Pisa, then La Spezia. Parking was very difficult to find, and it was just as difficult to know if one was parking in a no parking zone. Pisa was most worthy of note for more than one reason. And you can't go to Pisa without taking a photo of the Leaning Tower. We took many hysterically funny photos, mostly ones that made it appear we were holding up the tower to prevent it from falling. After, en route to Cinque Terre, we stopped for vino tasting at Punto Vendita and stayed at Green Quiet of Marvica, which is essentially an Italian Motel 6, but was surprisingly not too bad.

The next night, we stayed at Hotel Le Rotonde by Lake Massaciuccoli. The most memorable moment was my getting separated from my friends for nearly two hours. The short version...I was dropped off by the sign for the hotel. Oddly enough it didn't say "20 Kilometers", so we assumed it was actually within walking distance. I got out to find it on foot while my friends searched for parking as there were no available spaces nearby. Nearly two hours later we finally found each other, only to discover we did, in fact, still have 20 kilometers to go to get to our destination--go figure.

On Sunday, we took the rail to Cinque Terre and explored the five villages, including the beaches. Little did we know that once we got to the rail stop in Corniglia, we had to climb up 388 steps to reach the actual village. Seriously, every forty or so steps we'd reach a landing and take a long breather before continuing. If we weren't in shape before the trip, we certainly were moving in that direction after! Good thing going down the stairs was much easier.

On Monday, we drove further up the coast through Genova and then took the Autotrade to Milan/MXP. The grand finale night we stayed at Moxy by Marriott. The Hotel provided transport to the airport and off we went back to the good ole U.S.A. But one last adventure awaited—we were greeted with the parking ticket we managed to escape in Italy—what a relief to split it three ways.

The good news is, despite the adventures and mishaps along the way, our friendships remained intact and we had a fun and memorable experience of a lifetime. But I did learn a few lessons along the way:

1. Italians will quite literally go out of their way to help you.

2. They also take their wine very seriously!

3. Everything is 20 kilometers further than it seems.

4. And, last but not least, don't ever mess with the driver!

Adventures of a "Miss"aligned Roadtrip

By Holly Melby

It was Friday the 13th, 1998. Despite the ominous date, I was feeling nothing but luck. My bosses (I had three, just like the main character in Office Space) granted my request to take a half-day. I pulled my office door closed behind me looking forward to kicking off the Valentine's Day celebrations a little early. My feet moved like lightning down the condominium development flight of stairs, and I forcefully pushed open the door, gasping for a second as the brisk, February air whipped across my face. I tossed my purse onto the cloth-covered passenger seat of my red Pontiac Sunbird and turned the key in the ignition. The cold engine reluctantly coughed to life. I swear, even my car must've wondered why it lived in Illinois! Music blasted through the somewhat blown speakers–likely some classic like " Mo' Money Mo' Problems" that I probably rapped along passionately with, even though I had absolutely no money and no problems.

Navigating my way down the familiar streets of the Chicago northwest suburbs that I called home, I was eager to get to my destination. My boyfriend of three years was driving down from his dorm in Wisconsin to pick me up for a surprise Valentine's date. My assumption was that he was going to whisk me away to downtown Chicago, and I was eager to hear what he had in store for us. Not the most romantic perhaps, but I imagined us doing something super unique and service-oriented like passing out water bottles outside the Bulls game or giving heart-shaped chocolates to unsuspecting passersby. My guess couldn't have been more wrong.

When he arrived at my third floor apartment, he let himself into the front door that I had left unlocked for him. He found me in the bedroom I shared with my roommate, still scrambling to get ready for our date. Per usual, finding a piece of carpet to step on was rare, as every square inch of the room was covered in clothes, papers, and whatever random items my roommate must've haphazardly chucked around the room. It looked like I lived with Oscar the Grouch.

Pausing from reapplying a fresh coat of Cover Girl foundation, I greeted him with a kiss. He gave me a shy smirk and a large manila envelope. I had no idea what it was, but I felt like Ed McMahon had just told me I won the National Clearinghouse Sweepstakes. There was a handwritten note on the front: "This is my attempt at being more spontaneous." He had apparently listened to me when we recently had one of those relationship conversations where I told him I needed more adventure in my life. I smiled curiously, wondering what his cryptic message meant.

Eager to solve the mystery, I undid the metal clasps, being careful not to snap one off. It was stuffed full of information about New York City. Brochures. Maps. Research he'd printed off about things to do. I filed through it quickly trying to make sense of it all (and secretly looking for some plane tickets) when he asked, "Wanna go?" He explained that he had gassed up the car and packed a cooler full of snacks in preparation for an epic road trip. One raise of my eyebrows to confirm his sincerity, and I was in! I threw some clothes in a bag, grabbed my zippered CD case, and us free-spirits left the Midwest bound for The Big Apple!

At 19 and 20, we felt super grown-up. Our maturity was obvious too, because the used coupe that we were traveling in was not a complete beater, and our credit cards weren't

100% maxed out just yet. With our printed Mapquest directions and a free State Farm atlas in hand, we were on our way, just two cell phone-less dreamers headed to the city that never sleeps a la Harry and Sally!

Always ready for some deep, thought-provoking conversation, I kept my *IF* book close at hand. It contained conversation starters that helped us kill time on the 13-hour drive. We noshed on diagonally-cut ham sandwiches as we answered provocative questions like, 'If you could eliminate any one type of insect permanently from the earth, what would you get rid of?' Obviously, this was a short-lived conversation as there is only one right answer–centipedes.

At one particular gas station stop, we were hit up by two decorative-sashed Girl Scouts standing by their fully stocked table of beloved cookies. "Would you like to buy some Girl Scout cookies," they slowly said in unison, like they belonged in a horror film. *Uh, no, Poltergeist twins. I just want to make it to the toilet before I pee my pants.* My inner dialogue can be rudely curt, but instead I politely uttered, "Um, no thanks," and I shimmied past hearing them repeat their creepy anthem to the next sucker who just wanted to pay for his gas. I did my business, picked out some cheddar cheese Combos and Reese's Pieces with my traveling companion, and attempted to leave when we were assaulted by their monotone duet again, "Would you like to buy some Girl Scout cookies?" The last syllable in their aggressive sales pitch had a sing-songy ascent that got stuck in our heads causing us to say it repeatedly while we noshed on the Caramel De-lites we were talked into.

My beau had a fancy-schmancy six disc CD player that plugged into the lighter and balanced between us on the center console while it spun tunes. We took turns DJing which simply involved rotating out the handful of albums we happened to have with us. But without question, singer-songwriter Tracy Chapman's debut album played more than any other on that adventure. And appropriately, her hit single "Fast Car" is the ditty we sang along with the most on that road trip across the country.

Once we rolled into town, we headed straight to the Empire State Building. Unlike the romantic Sleepless in Seattle cute meet-up, our experience was rather anticlimactic. It was treacherously frigid on the iconic 86th floor, so we didn't take in the fantastic view for long. But despite our short time at our destination, we did manage to have a stranger kindly snap a shot of us. Our red noses and frozen smiles perfectly captured the uncomfortable windy moment before we bolted back inside for warmth.

A quick potty break at the Golden Arches, and then we were off to find some proper dinner. With a meal budget of about five bucks, we simply stopped at the first sit-down joint we could find. It happened to be a hole-in-the-wall Chinese restaurant with an uncomfortable ambiance and questionable shrimp. It wasn't good. At all. And yet, it was incredibly memorable and strangely romantic.

After giggling over our fortune cookies (because isn't every statement funnier when you add "naked" to the end?), we hopped back into the car before our parking meter expired and began navigating our way around Manhattan again. Suffice it to say, Midwesterners have no business being behind the wheel on the streets of New York. It all just happened so fast, and before we knew it we took a wrong turn and were dropping $7 on a bridge headed to Queens. Then we had to turn around and pay the same amount just to get back to where we were supposed to be. In a matter of a few minutes, I had tossed more than my nine-to-five hourly wage into the toll basket. We must've thrown our patience in right along with the cash, because our tone toward each other changed from passionate to pissy in a New York minute. It didn't take long for us to decide that we were insane for thinking we could take on the city and started heading back to the cornfields of Illinois where we rightly belonged.

25 years later, that boyfriend is now my husband. It's possible that we've lasted this long because that was our first and last long cross country road trip. However, we do look back on those memories fondly and have even commemorated it each year by maintaining an annual Valentine's Day tradition of enjoying Asian food. Multiple times we have returned to NYC, always via airplane. And never do we come across a table full of Girl Scout cookies without reminiscing about that adventurous trip!

The "Miss"taken Adventures of Death at the Black Sand Beach

By Lang Netzler

Have you heard of Maui's famous black sand beach, named Honokalani? It is very historically important for Hawaiians, and there are various legends about this place. The black sand beach is considered sacred by the Hawaiian people. Google says it was formed by lava flows that have cooled, hardened, and then fractured into tiny pieces by the relentless battering of the ocean waves over thousands of years. This is why you will see a variety of sand: rounded, smoothed pebbles, coarse, and in some areas, fine black sand.

Well, I had not heard of it, until one day...

My husband and I fell in love with Maui. After our first visit, "we" (meaning my husband) would always be on the lookout for deals and packages. In 2011, Costco offered an irresistible deal that we booked for our 4-year anniversary. My husband is half Samoan and half Japanese. I am half Chinese and half Cambodian. We blended in well and would go where the locals go to eat, shop, swim, and hang out. One of the locals shared about the famous Road to Hana. Charles and I looked at each other and thought, "Why not?!" Into our rental Jeep, and off we went.

It was a beautiful sunny day. With all the windows down, my hair was flowing in the soft, summer breeze. My husband was driving, listening to and singing country music. The Road to Hana is a long and difficult drive on a narrow, super windy mountain road. It is a 64-mile route that takes a tourist eight hours to drive. It is "only" a 3-hour commute for the locals. As a courtesy, it is suggested to let the locals speed past you, so they can get to work or home. This road has many pullouts to waterfalls, caves, gardens, pools, beaches, and hiking trails through the tropical rainforest. One of the stops had a sign that reads, "Black Sand Beach". We were intrigued. We had never been to a black sand beach before. We thought, "When in Rome...", so we went.

It was a quaint, private cove. The sand was pitch black and easy to walk on. The soft waves were very inviting and there were other people swimming.

Freeze...Let me add a note here. Charles can swim, but I cannot. Because of this, I would only play in the shallow end of the ocean while my husband would swim everywhere. OK, back to the story.

I followed Charles into the water. I stopped at the section where the water was only waist deep. Charles pulled my hand and tried to get me to go further. As he was pulling me deeper into the ocean, inch by inch, he tried to assure me, "Come on, the water is not that deep. You'll be fine." Before I realized it, my feet were no longer touching the ground.

Freeze... To tell you the truth, I don't quite remember the exact details of the events right before and after I realized that my feet were no longer touching the ocean floor.

Panic and fear set in. *What was happening?* I attempted to grab and cling to Charles. But every time I tried to get a hold of him, he would push me away. I don't quite remember if I was able to tell him that I was drowning, that I couldn't touch the bottom, or that I needed help. And after he repeatedly pushed me away, anger was also setting in. I was doggy-paddling to the rhythm of my pounding heartbeat. I was trying my best to keep my head above water. I saw other people swimming, but I was not getting anywhere close to them or the shore. My thoughts were all over the place. I had no desire to die, especially not this way.

It was then that my ears heard a faint cry for help from Charles. I suddenly realized that Charles was drowning, too. A different set of fear reoriented my thoughts to cry for help as well. Surprisingly, I had not been swallowing any of the ocean and was able to scream out, "Help!" I'm not quite sure if I continued to scream or if Charles was able to yell, but I saw people coming our way. With a quick sequence of events, we were sitting on the beach, recovering our breath and our minds.

I was just sitting on the warm, fine, black sand, looking over the ocean, and replaying what just happened in my mind, over and over again. There were people checking on us and offering us water. On my right, I heard my husband explaining the event to the strangers that just saved our lives:

> "Yeah, all of a sudden, I was pulled under by the current. I was trying to swim towards the shore, but the current kept me back. I was getting exhausted. Then, I felt Lang kept trying to hold onto me. I kept trying to push her towards the shore, but we were both stuck in the

current. I was having a hard time yelling for help. Every time I tried, I would get a good dose of ocean water instead. I was finally able to get something out, and I think that's when Lang yelled for help, too."

As my husband was rinsing his mouth of the saltwater taste, my paradigm shifted. He wasn't being a jerk. He wasn't trying to kill me.

According to Google's definition, I also wasn't drowning. I was not suffocated or submerged by the water–I was treading it. My breathing ability was not hindered by the water–it was affected by the fight-or-flight response of my nervous system. So, I wasn't drowning in water; I was drowning in fear. Fear convinced me that I was going to die because I didn't know how to swim. Fear added unneeded stress, in a situation that would have resulted in the same outcome with or without it. Regardless, I was grateful that my body went into auto-pilot survival-mode and sustained my life, despite my mind being frozen in fear-mode. And in the end, the only thing that died that day was my fear of drowning.

As we were walking back towards the jeep, backtracking the way that we came in, we noticed a sign. It was a warning sign about the dangers of drowning due to sudden changes in the ocean current. HA! That sign would have been much more useful if it had gigantic neon lights around it.

Who am I kidding?! Like it would have mattered! Even if we had seen the sign on our way in, the sequence of events would have still happened the same way. We would still have jumped in without thinking twice. Oh well. Back in the jeep, and the journey continued. Next stop: The Seven Sacred Pools of Maui!

Adventures of a "Miss"interpreted Life Plan

By Ashley Huyck

Never in my life would I have thought I would be sitting in the back of a cop car with one shoe on. Then again, never in my life did I imagine being in a relationship with someone who would hurt me. And never in my life did I think I would have to call 911 because mine and my daughter's lives were in danger.

When we first met a year prior, it all felt normal and exciting. He made me feel wanted, beautiful, and important. There were dinner dates, weekend adventures, movies, and inside jokes. I didn't notice the red flags of control and signs of losing myself.

I was a strong woman who had worked hard for my career and what I had accomplished. At the time, I had been a teacher for nine years. Alongside my career, I had started a jewelry business and was driven to eventually make it my primary source of income.

He loved that I was motivated, educated, and working on building a business. Likewise, I liked that he was also an entrepreneur–we had that in common. We would share business ideas and talk about ways that we could support each other's visions.

Flash forward to the current me sitting in the police vehicle. I couldn't have been further from the driven, independent woman that I once was. The questions started flooding my thoughts: *What is going to happen now? Would I lose my house? Would I lose custody of my daughter? Would I lose my job? Would I ever be able to teach again?*

How did I end up here?

When we arrived at the police station, the police officers opened the car door to let me out. The female officer looked at my feet. I had one sandal on. "Where is your other shoe?" she asked.

I glanced at my feet, looked her in the eyes, and quietly said, "Probably where he choked me." This was the first time that a look of "Oh shit, we messed up." washed over her face. My other sandal was removed. I walked barefoot into the station where they led me to a room with a computer, a couple of desks, and a few chairs.

Once again, I was questioned about what happened. And, once again, I recalled the events of the evening. They began to dig deeper into my story and ask more detailed questions. It was four in the morning, and I was exhausted. I sat there in my shorts and t-shirt with no shoes on while they demanded to know why *I* had hit *him*; why I had *lied* to them about the marks on my neck.

The officer stated I was being charged with a felony of burglary and a few misdemeanors. The only word that I heard was "felony". It rang in my ears like the screaming siren of a passing fire truck, loud and repeating. Immediately, I started crying. Uncontrollable tears rolled down my face—the silent cry, where you can't stop the tears as they just drip off your face, down your neck, and onto your shirt.

The female officer looked me in the eyes and said, "You'll be okay. This probably won't have that much of an impact on your life overall." *Bitch, what?* I was probably not her typical arrest. I had a 9-year teaching career, owned my own home, and had a 6-month-old daughter. It most definitely was going to impact my life in numerous ways.

The next step of being booked required taking all my personal belongings: my necklace, hair tie, phone, or anything else I had on me, and making a record of them. When I reached up to take my earrings off I realized that I was also missing an earring. Not just any earrings, but my favorite Kate Spade, multicolored, sparkle studs.

The female officer looked at me blankly and reluctantly asked, "Where is your other earring?"

"Probably where he choked me," I stated yet again.

For the second time, the look in her eyes told me, "Oh shit, we really messed up." But it was too late. Unfortunately, there are no get-out-of-jail-free cards in real life.

The one personal item I was able to keep were my glasses. I was extremely thankful to have them so that I could see and observe, but quite honestly, there was nothing about this experience that I wanted to remember.

After hours of sitting in a hard, plastic chair, my name was called to go back to change my clothes and be taken to wherever this hell hole had for me next. I held a scratchy blanket close to my chest while I dragged my feet in my fabulous jail-loaned, orange-rubber, slide-on sandals, and down the hall we went to the pods where all the cells were located.

A little while later, I was laying in my cell with my detoxing cellmate. I was on the bottom bunk with the scratchy blanket covering me, trying to warm up. I don't know if I was cold or just shivering from not knowing what was going to happen next.

Time dragged on. It was hard to know what time it was, because I couldn't see the clock in the main area of the pod. I finally figured out that the guard passed our door every 15 minutes, so with a pen they gave me and the piece of paper that had my personal items on it, I started keeping track of the time. Every 15 minutes I put a dot. Every four dots was an hour.

It was so hard not to let my thoughts spiral out of control while sitting in a jail cell. So I just kept praying. Praying that God would help me breathe, and, mostly, that He would give me peace. In those moments, I could feel His presence with me. In my darkest hour, He was there, holding me. As a sense of calm washed over me, my thoughts started to change. I kept hearing a voice tell me, "You will use this experience for other women. You will always be a teacher—not always in a traditional sense, but your classroom will have no walls."

In that jail cell, I found peace. How I navigate my comeback and rebuild my life will be a beacon of hope for other women in need. I didn't know at the time what that would look like. But I did know that the opportunities would come if I trusted the process. And, to this day, it still gives me hope that no matter what happens, my mess can be someone else's message.

I was released from jail the next day. My souvenirs were a protection order against me regarding my daughter's dad and a court date set for two weeks out. Lucky me. I was the victim—yet I was also the one with the criminal charges.

As the months went by and my case moved along, I was offered a plea deal: if I followed the judge's orders, took domestic violence therapy, and completed probation, my charges would be deferred. They wouldn't go away, but my record would show that I was never convicted. My lawyer and I decided that this was the best-case scenario for me.

A few weeks after accepting my plea, a letter arrived from the Colorado Department of Education—the big dogs of teacher licensure and qualification. The letter stated that with my felony charges, I could either go on trial before the Board of Education or surrender my teaching license. This was soul-crushing. What I had worked so hard for was going to be taken away from me. Nine years of teaching, four years of college, countless teacher development classes, creating curriculum, long school days, staff meetings, parent emails, and everything else was wasted.

Or so my mind was telling me.

I sat with the decision for a couple of days to figure out what I wanted to do. *Should I hire another lawyer?* I already had a criminal lawyer and a family lawyer for custody. *What if I went in front of the board and they still decided that I would be an unfit teacher? Is teaching even what I really want to do with my life? Or was this the opportunity to do something else?*

I'd hit ground zero, but was this a blessing in disguise to run my business full-time? I had always wanted to do what I truly love. I started to think that this unfortunate event could actually be my permission slip to create the life that I'd always dreamt of. Yet I also knew the financial responsibility of caring for my daughter would fall completely on my shoulders. Counting on child support was not something I was banking on knowing her father's track record when it came to his older child.

My dad owns a business and has always been an advocate for me to have my own. When I saw him at a family gathering, I knew I had to ask him for advice. If he was able to create a business that supported our family with four kids, I could support my mini-me and myself. I remember standing in the middle of the street saying goodbye and he told me, "If you want to surrender your teaching license and build your business, do it. Don't look back. Put everything into building your business."

So that's exactly what I did. I surrendered my license and went back to school for graphic design. I was finally starting my business.

In the beginning, all I had was a laptop, a camera, and my baby girl. But I knew I had all the tools that I needed to succeed. If I didn't know how to do something, I could figure it out myself. As a student of YouTube and Google, I could even find a video or step-by-step tutorial to teach me what I needed.

And so I became a photographer and graphic designer. I began building websites for small, women-owned businesses. I quickly learned how to use social media to market myself.

As I started creating these brands and websites, I quickly realized that most of these women needed even more support after their website was completed. They needed a mentor to show them how to get clients and set pricing for products or services. And the one thing I saw most of my clients struggle with was the mindset of a successful business owner.

That was when I created my first online course. I was going to show women how to start a business and take them from idea to profit, giving them the power of financial stability and flexibility to be the mom they were meant to be while following the passions of their heart.

I taught the course for the first time in January of 2021, where four women dove into their ideas and built a business that they had been wanting for months, if not years. The eight-week course gave them the resources and tools to stop overthinking and finally start their business.

That fall, it was put on my heart that it was time to start using my journey of loss and self-discovery to help other women. I began volunteering at a local nonprofit to serve other single moms. When I met the director and staff, I explained my story and how I was now running my own online business. Unbeknownst to me, the nonprofit had a grant opportunity to present a program idea to be funded. In our meeting, the director explained the opportunity and asked if I had any outside-of-the-box ideas that would help moms overcome poverty. It took all I had for my body to not start jumping up and down at this opportunity that was just effortlessly prepared for me. I knew that it was divinely designed for me to be there at that exact moment, to present my business program and start helping single moms launch businesses of their own.

The program officially launched in February of 2022, with 11 women meeting in the classroom of a church. I was teaching again. Just three years after surrendering my license, I was finally back in my element, designing curriculum and impacting women that would model strength and resilience to their children; helping them break the cycle of poverty for themselves and their families.

Everyone experiences a loss in their life. It may not be as extreme as being arrested and losing your career along with your shoes. But we all lose something of value to us: a break-up, a friendship, a job, a diagnosis, or any human experience that forces an individual to rebuild or heal.

If there is one thing that I would love for you to take from my story is that even at your darkest moment, when you are wondering "why is this happening to me?", remind yourself to reframe your thoughts. A simple shift in perspective leaves behind that victim mentality and re-establishes your power to rise above.

So rather than having a pity party for one, the next time you are facing a loss in your own life, instead ask yourself: "*How* is this happening *for* me?" Because even when a situation seems hopeless, we really do have more control than we think.

Never "Miss" the Opportunity for an Adventure

By Taunya Kepple

I've had many opportunities to travel for work and pleasure. Whether traveling alone or with my partner, with family or friends, I have always embraced each moment.

I've been on Dutch and German Navy destroyer ships as far east as the Madeira Islands in Portugal and as far West as the highest point of a mountain in Kauai, HI. I have traveled alone to Europe for four weeks at a time for work, including a time when I was 32 weeks pregnant. On that particular trip I was headed to Amsterdam, The Netherlands. On the way, I had stopped over for a day in Chicago, IL and took a bus to visit my grandma. I'll never forget how many times she told me how proud and in awe of me she was, as an African American woman, traveling alone, pregnant, and overseas. That was unheard of in her youth and especially in the prior generation.

Looking back at the 31 states and 9 countries I've been blessed to see and experience, my most favorite place in the world is Moab, Utah! I have only been there twice, but each time was a solo "me, myself, and I" trip that my soul truly needed. I found that the scenery from the drive along Highway 128 along the Colorado River to the breathtaking views at Dead Horse State Park (setting of a famous scene from my all-time favorite movie *Thelma and Louise*) is something that brings me inner peace. I strongly recommend every girl, at some point in their life, also finds at least one solo destination.

"Traveling alone will be the scariest, most liberating, life-changing experience of your life. Try it at least once!"-- Unknown Author

"Miss"cellaneous Adventures of a Solo Explorer

By Teresa Morey

This year was a whirlwind. My family dealt with a lot of change in a very short time. My husband returned from being away due to a military separation for eight months. He retired after 20 years, and we were able to decide where we would like our 'forever home' to be. We chose to stay in Colorado for many reasons, among them being it was his last station in the U.S. and the place my son and I called home while he was away. This led us both to starting new jobs in totally new fields. We decided to sell our current home and buy a new one, changing the school for our son. I also began helping my friends promote their local businesses through social media in my free time.

This everyday adventure story comes from a military spouse whose closest friends are geographically not so close. The older I get, the busier I am and the faster time passes. I've always wanted to go visit my friends but felt that there was always something holding me back—holidays, birthdays, money, time, life—the list of excuses goes on. Finally, with the support of my husband, I decided that I had to make the time to just do it. I needed to go see my friends. I originally planned to fly because I wanted to stop in Alabama, Florida, Mississippi, and Texas. Though each of the places are relatively close together, the cost of flying and renting a vehicle proved more expensive than driving my own vehicle from Colorado. I also didn't want my son to miss too much school so, the plan was set: a solo road trip for me.

I left the day after Thanksgiving. My first stop was to see one of my very best friends, April. She lives in Tuscaloosa, Alabama. We first met in England where we lived for about three years. Then we both ended up in New Mexico in a remote town for seven more. Living somewhere you wouldn't have chosen for *seven years* really solidifies a friendship. I was really lucky to have lived so close to her for so long. She became my personal cheerleader—encouraging and loyal. She recently had a baby and I wanted to make it out to see her and her new family. I was able to surprise her with the help of her significant other. It worked—she had no idea! We were able to go have dinner and drinks and then brunch the next morning before I had to leave. Even though I only spent about a day with her, we were able to connect and catch up, and I finally got to meet her new baby.

My next stop was only a few hours down the road in Dothan, Alabama to see my friend Hayley. We originally met in 2018 when we both worked for the same insurance office. She wasn't in Colorado very long before she moved away, but we quickly formed a close friendship. Hayley surprised me with a visit last summer and really wanted me to come see her. She was actually the reason that spurred me to make this trip before she had to move again. And I'm glad I did. I was able to see her daughter, her new house and her five cats. We had a relaxing time eating, watching shows and just catching up.

The next part of my trip was a little more spontaneous. I had originally planned to go to Destin, Florida, but decided to make a few extra stops along the way. First, I met one of my former coworkers at a coffee shop in Lynnhaven. From there, I wasn't sure if I should stop at my old employers' office in Santa Rosa Beach. I used to be an administrative assistant to the owner of an engineering firm, and I was a little hesitant as it had been so many years since we had even talked. You know how fast life moves—with time and distance people are often forgotten. I wasn't even sure they would want to see me. But boy was I wrong. I lucked out and my old boss, Dean, his wife, Tracey, and his co-owner, Dexter, were in, and we were able to catch up. Our short visit reminded me how much I missed that work family and how I felt I really belonged. I can't put into words how much this meant to me.

I stayed at the Hilton in Destin, Florida. The view from my room was amazing. I could see the Gulf of Mexico, with the sun sparkling on the translucent green water, and smell the salty air. I kept the door open so that I could hear the waves as they crashed against the beach. I went to dinner with my niece at a restaurant that I used to love when I lived there. Unfortunately, the reality didn't live up to my memory this time. After dinner I drove by all of the old haunts—my old high school, AJ's bar that my friends and I used to frequent, my childhood home. Many places were still there, but they weren't the same.

The following day I woke up extra early so that I could watch the sunrise on the beach. I stopped by my favorite artist gallery on 30A, Justin Gafrey. I didn't have the budget to purchase a new painting, but I was able to admire his works and purchase a few kits that he has curated to do at home. (I still have not opened them.)

A couple friends discovered I was still in the area so I agreed to meet with each of them. I met Cornellius for coffee. I had not seen him since high school. I've never been to a reunion, so we reminisced and spoke of what happened to friends since then. He told me how he always thought I was so kind. It was a bit eye opening as I knew we were friendly, but I didn't know that he thought so highly of me back then. I think it helped me realize that my view of myself was far more critical than what others saw. Then I met with my old coworker, Marek, for Thai in Fort Walton Beach. We talked about work, our families, and life since I left.

On to see my sister in Ocean Springs, Mississippi. I got to her place late as planned and immediately went to sleep. The next day she took the day off to spend with me. We went to get manicures, had lunch, and worked on going through our mother's belongings. The day flew by as I helped her around her house. She took me out to dinner in Biloxi at a place called Adventures. Afterwards, we went to a casino to have a few drinks. I played on a slot machine and won $200!

Next stop: Houston, Texas, for an overnight visit with my best friend, Lynette, who I met in sixth grade. We grew up about a block away from each other and went on to high school and even the University of Florida together. At one point, we even worked together. She has *known* me—through all of my phases as a preteen and into adulthood. She has witnessed my relationships from my first boyfriend to my husband. She's always been there.

I honestly can't remember the last time I saw Lynette. I think it was about eight years ago when I was driving through on another road trip. Crazy how things have changed since then. But once the kids were sleeping, we started talking and it felt like when we were back in high school talking about boys or friends or whatever was on our youthful minds. Only this time we were talking about our parents and raising our own families. We spent so much time talking, before we knew it, it was 2am. I had to head back home the next day and planned to leave by 6am. Oops! But I did manage to get on the road by 7am.

As I drove over fourteen hours back to Colorado, I reflected on the reconnections I made in this short, ten-day journey. If I could have done anything differently, I simply would have spent more time at each place. Everywhere I went was just too short. But I'm so glad I did it. That quick trip recharged my spirit. I didn't even realize just how much I had missed my friends and family. I didn't know how much I missed where I grew up. I now understand the connection Scarlet O'Hara had to the land in *Gone with the Wind*. Scarlet knew that the land was waiting for her–she always had a place to go back to, and I do too. I realized I need to make more time to see the important people in my life as often as I can. As cliche as it is, life *is* short. We need to seize the moments we have and make time for the important people in our lives.

Adventures of a "Miss"placed Dreamer

By Maggie Rasch

Time is the most precious thing we have. It's fleeting, and we have no control over how quickly it passes. Once it's gone, we never get it back. What we do have is a choice to either waste those moments or fill them with experiences that become our life's treasures.

Sometimes we don't realize we're in the process of creating an extraordinary moment while it's actually happening. For example, I'm sitting here on a snowy, January morning with one of my daughters, looking at pictures of when I was a baby. How did the time go by in the blink of an eye? Thankfully, photos are a window into the past. Mine are black and white, but the memories are filled with vibrant colors as I relive them. I look through these photos and regale stories from my childhood—my past comes back vividly.

I think I was a cute baby. I had dirty blonde hair, but you would never know it now. As I grew, my hair changed to red and then it eventually transitioned to the almost black that I still sport to this day. Memories come flooding back. Life wasn't always easy as the oldest daughter in my family. I had a lot of responsibilities including being in charge of my six younger siblings. I do have an older brother, but being a girl in those days meant I had a certain number of gender-specific duties.

My dad was very strict--even mean sometimes. But that was probably his way of being protective of his family. As a proud Mexican immigrant, he had to learn things the proper way. So, his children, of course, had to learn things properly as well. He was a big city guy from San Antonio. My mom was a country girl from South Dakota with Native American roots. Back in those days, Native Americans were referred to as "Indians". They couldn't have been more opposite.

My mom was a very intelligent woman, wise beyond her years. When she married my dad, she quickly learned how to become a Mexican wife: cooking traditional dishes and speaking Spanish. But, for some reason she never learned to drive. She told stories about how she had to do it one time during an emergency, but it wasn't something that ever happened again. She was fully dependent on my dad and then became physically dependent on her children as health issues disabled her later in life. She always had big dreams, but something held her back. I'm a lot like my mother in that way. I miss her and my dad.

Anxiety isn't something I acquired as an adult—it runs in my family. I grew up having a lot of phobias. I'm not entirely sure where they came from, but I remember suffering from worry through even my earliest memories. In my hometown of Kadoka, SD nobody paid attention to me. In school, I was always the last one picked in sports. I was very shy and didn't have confidence in myself, so I didn't have many friends. I felt like I was looked down on because of my dark complexion. Being Mexican and "Indian" and not fitting into either world made me want to escape into my imagination. Since I was poor for most of my life, the next best thing was always reading. I used to go to the library and check out books. That's where I found my love for adventure.

Another escape was my passion for art. I knew I was good at it from an early age. I had dreams of going to art school and becoming a fashion designer. In the beginning, I practiced my craft by designing clothes for my paper dolls. But once I became an adult, many years went by and I felt uninspired to create, so the passion faded away.

Instead of going to art school, I had various jobs over the years. My first job was working as a waitress at a restaurant in my small town of Kadoka. I was 14. I had originally applied to be a dishwasher because I was so shy, but I didn't know how to say no when they asked me to be a waitress instead. On my very first day, one of my customers was mean to me and I had a good cry in the bathroom afterwards. Working there ended up being the best experience I could have imagined. I learned a lot of life lessons that I store in the back of my head. The next summer I became the salad girl. I caught on quickly and helped the cooks with prepping by the time I was 17. I was feeling pretty confident until I cut myself with a meat slicer and was rushed to the hospital.

We moved a couple of times because my dad was in construction building bridges on Interstate 90, which runs across the entire state of South Dakota and most of the country. After Kadoka, we moved to Box Elder, on the outskirts of Rapid City, where Ellsworth Air Force base is located. It was 1962, and we lived in a cabin that summer. But two years later we moved to a trailer park in Rapid City, and things really started to change for me.

Moving there was a culture shock. It was a military town. After all the years of feeling invisible suddenly people started paying attention to me—it was odd. At that time, I didn't like school, so I stopped attending and my dad decided to keep me at home. In those days, you could go to bars if you were with your parents, so one time I went to see a live band with my family. My sister ended up joining the band and instantly had an exciting life. I, on the other hand, was shy and not allowed to date. But one of the guys in the band, who was also in the Air Force, persistently pursued me. He asked me to marry him two months later--four more and we were married. My life was finally going to begin—I was going to have a family, travel and live out the exciting life I had always dreamed of!

As long as I can remember, I have had this sense of wonder when it comes to travel. Some people hate airports, but I really like them. They're special to me because they represent the start of an adventure. When my two oldest children were young, we got stationed in Guam. My husband had to fly ahead of us. Our flight was delayed, resulting in me flying alone with toddlers on an empty airplane. My husband didn't know what happened to us and became very worried. But despite being inexperienced and insecure, I felt an element of excitement in this unexpected adventure. I still tell the story to my kids to this day.

From there, every move was an adventure, for which the military did not disappoint. We relocated many times, ending up in Illinois, where I became a bartender in 1976. By this time, I had six kids and needed a friend to babysit so I could work. The first bar I worked at was called Locomotion (funny how things sometimes ironically represent your life). My husband got me the job. I didn't want to do it at first, but it wasn't my choice. We needed the money, so there wasn't much I could do except try to get through it. It taught me how to come out of my shell and talk to people. I think this was when I truly started discovering my independence.

As a natural caretaker, I have always done jobs attending to others. I was a maid for many years as my kids were growing up in Rapid City. But eventually, I went back to the food service industry as a breakfast attendant at a hotel. I never gave up on my dreams to make my own money though. From those early years of wanting to become a fashion designer, I always had an entrepreneurial spirit. My husband and I delved into direct sales at one point and tried our hands at selling Amway. Over time he lost interest in that plan, but I continued to keep things going for a bit. Eventually, we both decided to go back to our musical roots and started a family band with our kids.

Our band, Family Affair, performed locally, and eventually toured in nearby states. This was the best of both worlds for me! I've always loved art and music, but traveling to new places was a huge bonus! I consider myself to have the heart of a gypsy. Wanderers and vagabonds have always fascinated me. This stems from my intense longing to explore the world. I've always admired the people that get to do this in their life. I especially enjoy road trips. When my kids were little, we drove twelve hours from Rapid City to Milwaukee, Wisconsin for an annual family trip to visit my mother-in-law. We played tourist no matter if it was a gas station, rest stop or restaurant that we stopped at along the way. The whole trip was a fun time because the family was together making memories.

Children are a gift–we have to remember that. They do drive us crazy at times. But there's no greater love than what you have for your child. I have ten great loves: five boys and five girls. I'm in awe at how talented my kids are. Most of them have musical and artistic abilities of some sort. I've had the pleasure of watching them grow up on a stage and develop their skills over many years. I get chills every time I hear my children play and sing. I still love singing too. Karaoke is definitely a family favorite when we all get together.

If you're a parent, you know that there are times where this love amounts to a lot of suffering too. I think you worry even more about them after they grow up and become adults. When they're young, you try to keep them safe and at home. After they grow up, you must trust that you provided all the tools they need to take care of themselves. I worry about my loves. I even watch the weather all over the country, so I know my kids that live in other cities are doing well.

Some of them have it together the majority of the time. And some of them...well, let's just say life hasn't been the easiest. My youngest son called while we were sitting here looking at pictures and reminiscing. He's currently in jail. But even while he's locked up, we're lightheartedly telling stories from when he was little. He had been missing for several months because he had violated his probation and was on the run. I had to file a missing person's report—a very disheartening thing to do when you're a parent. I didn't know if he was alive or dead. Strangely, it's a comfort for him to finally be in jail where at least I know he's safe. His older brother unexpectedly and tragically passed away a little over a year ago. I've experienced some terrible things in the seventy-six years that I've been on this earth—but that was by far the hardest thing I've ever gone through.

After Michael passed away, I started to delve back into drawing. I wanted to honor his memory and decided to draw his portrait, just like all the drawings I used to do before my passion faded away. The creative juices have finally come back. My hobby brings me joy, and I want to leave something of myself behind for my children and my grandchildren—a legacy of sorts, I suppose. I've been designing unique projects, and I want my kids to remember their mom created something special for them.

I am so grateful for all the experiences I've been blessed with over the years. But time waits for no one, and there are still so many things I want to do. I have a combination of an "I can do it" and "I'm too afraid to do it" way of thinking. It's a conundrum. But I've never given up hope. For instance, I've always wanted a tattoo. But for some reason I've never gotten one. Probably for the same reason I've held myself back from doing a lot of things. My youngest son has tattoos on his fingers that I'm not exactly a fan of. He gave them to *himself*! I told him it's a bad idea to put a girlfriend's name on your body since you may not be together one day. Some ideas are best left in our minds and not on our bodies.

With that being said, I am starting to let go of the fear of the perception other people might have of me. I try to be present in the moment now. Dancing has always been a passion of mine. But I'm learning to stop worrying about looking like a fool in front of others. Instead, I get out there and have so much fun bringing out my inner child. After all, at the end of your life all you have are your memories. And I'm determined to have a treasure chest full of them.

Adventures of a "Miss"understood Gen Z

By Reese Walton

My mom has been getting on me about starting this story, so this is my attempt in doing so.

I think I'm a pretty typical teenager. I'm almost 18 years old. I'm still in high school. I hang out with my friends, use social media, and enjoy binging TV shows. I like doing bold makeup, getting my nails done, and dressing up occasionally as well. I have a nose ring and want other piercings and tattoos, which my parents aren't very fond of. I'm extremely close with my parents, but we don't always see eye-to-eye. My mom is very adventurous, outgoing, and open to almost any opportunity thrown her way; my dad is a stubborn, retired Air Force Special Agent who cares deeply for and is protective of his family. Both my parents have conservative views, while I have more liberal tendencies. This definitely results in differences of opinion and how we feel about certain events that occur in today's society.

Being a military brat, I moved around a lot when I was younger. I was born in Rapid City, South Dakota, which I have no memory of, because we moved to Florida when I was still a baby. Then we moved again, four years later, to England, where my first memories began. I grew up with two older brothers, Samuel and Mason. Samuel is five years older than me and Mason is two and-a-half years older, making me the youngest. I've always been closer with Samuel because he's very kind and easy-going. He also jokes around a lot. I wanted to be just like him when I was younger. Mason and I always fought when we were little, in the same way all siblings argue. But we get along better now. (Sometimes he still gets on my nerves, don't get me wrong...).

I remember when my only concerns in the world were my baby dolls and my best friends that I played with almost every day. I remember when I begged for a puppy for my fifth birthday, until my parents finally gave in. We got our family dog Abbey, who's still my best friend to this day. I remember being obsessed with horses and wishing I could have my own horse to ride to school. I remember riding bikes up and down my street every day. I remember how I screamed with excitement when I got an iPod Touch for Christmas. I remember how I lost my first tooth pretending to be a dog and picking up my stuffed animals with my mouth, and I remember being scared of the dark. I also remember when my parents told us we were going to be moving to Colorado. I was eight years old. I had never heard of "Colorado" before.

I've lived in Colorado, specifically Colorado Springs, longer than any other place. When we first moved here, I was sick for almost a week. Like, throwing up, feeling miserable, sick. So, that's my first memory of life in Colorado.

Since we moved here almost ten years ago, I've definitely grown into the person I am today. I met my best friend of eight years, Jada, in fourth grade when she was a new student, and I asked her if she wanted to play on the swings at recess. Despite having a few falling outs over the years, we've always managed to come back together.

We got another dog when I was nine—his name was Jax. He was the most hyper dog I have ever met and was always in need of attention. Abbey couldn't stand him, and they often got into little play fights. At this age, I was definitely a little boy-crazy and always had a crush on someone. I loved having sleepovers with my friends and making up dances with my cousin, Presley, that we'd perform for our huge family. We even bought matching outfits for one of our routines. She started crying, because she had become shy and nervous about performing in front of our family, so I consoled her, and we did our dance. It was amazing.

When I was 12, my parents surprised me with horseback riding lessons for my birthday, and my love for horses grew even more. I rode for almost three years before I quit, because I thought my trainer was mean when her harsh instructions would make me cry. Despite the tough times, I sometimes miss being a little kid when I think of these memories.

I was in middle school when I first began discovering who I was as a person and what I believed in. My main priorities were school, my friends, horseback riding, and my dogs. My family lived in a beautiful house, and I loved making little video skits in my room on an app called Musically, now famously known as TikTok.

But even though I was very grateful for the lifestyle I had, we weren't always happy at home. My brother Samuel joined the military, so he was gone for months in basic training. My parents were constantly fighting or arguing, which resulted in me feeling anxious a lot of the time. It eventually got to the point where I'd get bad anxiety even if they were just in a room alone together. I would cry, shake, and sometimes even hyperventilate. Whenever I'd hear them start fighting, I'd stop whatever I was doing just to listen. My friends encouraged me to ignore it, put in my earbuds, and listen to music to drown it out. But I couldn't. I had to listen and make sure everything turned out okay in the end. There were several instances in my childhood where I felt like I had to intervene in the fighting, because I feared the safety of one of them, and that's really heavy to deal with when you're young. By the time I was 13, I actually wanted my parents to separate and get a divorce. It may not sound great from my end, but sometimes adults don't understand that their fighting greatly affects the kids too. This experience in my life has definitely had an impact on me and my struggle with anxiety today.

My parents eventually got divorced when I was 14 years old, a freshman in high school. I remember the day my mom called me to tell me it was official. It was snowing outside, some day in October, and I was walking to my Spanish class. Even though I was relieved that the horrible cycle of fighting was over, I still felt like I wanted to cry. I knew that it was finally going to get better, but I still had a lot of life-altering changes coming my way.

It was shortly after my 15th birthday that COVID-19 became a big concern in the U.S. There was talk of schools being shut down due to the spread of the illness, and I remember thinking that I hoped our school would be one of them. I never thought it'd actually happen though. I remember feeling off that day for some reason, as I was sitting in my study hall class on the morning of March 13th– coincidentally Friday the 13th. My principal came over the intercom announcing that we'd have an extra week of spring break. That "extra week" turned into doing the rest of my freshman year and almost half of my sophomore year online. The first couple of weeks felt like a vacation. I got to sleep in, stay in bed all day, hangout with my dogs, and talk to my friends. I had recently become friends with a new student at our school that I considered my best friend at the time, so I was pretty content.

I've had crooked teeth my whole life, which other kids constantly bullied me for. One of the insults I remember the most was "horse teeth," and this obviously took a toll on my self-esteem. Around the end of May 2020, I got my wisdom teeth (and four other adult teeth) removed. I was so excited to start my journey into having straight teeth. A month after getting my wisdom teeth out, I got braces. I instantly sent a video to my best friend, showing her my new smile, which resulted in her laughing at me, saying that I didn't look good. Coming from my best friend, this obviously hurt my feelings. There had also been an instance before where her boyfriend had been making fun of me in a video, calling me ugly, in which she just played along and laughed with him. I had always been silent when situations like this happened, so I finally decided to stand up for myself and explained to her that her words made me feel bad. Even though I was proud of myself, this only resulted in her getting mad at me and calling me ugly to my face. I told her that I was hurt, I still loved her, and I thought she was beautiful despite her harsh words. Then I blocked her on all social media platforms. That was the day that I realized sometimes even the people you trust the most aren't always who they seem.

The same day, I ended up reconnecting with my best friend, Jada, from elementary school. It was around September of 2020. I was a sophomore at this point, and me and Jada hadn't been friends for a little over a year due to dumb middle school drama. We went to different high schools, so it's not like we saw each other around. One day we decided to hangout again. I went into my mom's room, asking her if Jada could sleep over, where she responded, "That's a little random, but okay." Jada got there, and it was honestly a little awkward, which was weird for us. But we quickly got comfortable again and were inseparable for the rest of sophomore year. At this point, she knew everything about me, and I knew everything about her. We bonded over normal teenage girl things (boys, school drama, etc). She helped me feel comfortable in figuring out what style I wanted for myself, and what kind of person I did and didn't want to be. I thought of her like a sister; we even fought like siblings at times.

However, my parents haven't always been fond of Jada. In April of 2021, I was sort of in my rebellious stage at 16. Jada and I (and another friend at the time) had made the decision to skip school. We all went to my house, and long story short, my mom came home on her lunch break and caught us in the act. She told my friends to leave, and I was grounded for over a month. This is when my parents started to think of her as a bad influence. Little did they know, skipping school was actually my idea. Anyway, that's the longest I've ever been grounded for something, and Jada and I distanced ourselves from each other for a while. Of course, we soon became friends again a couple months later.

The summer of 2021 brought a lot of changes for our family. My dad had already moved into his own place, while my mom, Mason, and I (and of course Abbey and Jax) still lived in the family home. Shortly after Mother's Day we put our house on the market to sell. And at the end of April, my mom came to the decision to rehome our dog Jax. I was devastated. He was always having accidents around the house and needed attention we couldn't always give him. I had never dealt with the loss of a pet before (besides my hamster when I was 11. R.I.P. Hammy), so I was taking it pretty hard. The day we sent him off to his new family, I sobbed as he left my arms, afraid that he would be scared and think that we'd abandoned him.

About a month later, we moved into our new (and current) house. The move was long and stressful. Overall, I was excited to have a new beginning and a new room, despite experiencing a bit of anxiety due to all of the recent changes. We moved right next to a different high school than the one I went to (like, it's a three minute walk to school). My mom was responsible for taking us to school in the morning, so she tried really hard to convince me to switch to this other school so that she could go to work earlier. I was stubborn and already felt like too much change was happening, so I was adamant about staying where I was. Jada had also just switched to my school, so I really didn't want to leave.

Around this time, my mom and I started doing a weekly tradition called Mother-Daughter Monday, where we would spend time together in some way every Monday, whether it was going out to eat, making dinner, watching a movie, etc. It was a nice way to ensure that we spent time together despite all the other things going on in our lives.

On a particular Mother-Daughter Monday, my cousin Jazzy called me saying it was urgent. I assumed it was probably dumb teenage girl stuff, because we tell each other everything in that regard. But instead she ended up telling me that our uncle, Michael, had been in an accident, that he was in the hospital, and it was uncertain if he was going to survive. Still, I didn't take it that seriously. I went upstairs to my mom's room where she was getting ready, and I told her what Jazzy had told me. She called one of her sisters, asked about the situation, and broke down in tears. That's when I knew that it actually was serious.

A few weeks later, we drove up to Rapid City, South Dakota, where almost our whole family lives, to attend Michael's funeral. I wasn't sure how to feel, because we've never experienced a death like this in our family. Although I was sad, I wasn't very close to Michael. I loved and cared about him, but I only saw him for a brief period every few years. During his funeral, I didn't expect myself to cry for these reasons. But I actually cried a lot. I cried for my family, my mom, and Michael's son, who I had never met until that day. Although the event itself was sad, it brought our whole family together, which I thought was kind of beautiful.

I ended up staying at my school for four months before I eventually switched. It had been a long semester of having to figure out rides to and from school, sometimes resulting in walking two miles home. I was nervous to start at a new school, but mostly excited for a fresh start. When I first got there, a part of me expected kids to go out of their way to introduce themselves and become friends with me, like how it was in elementary school. Obviously that didn't happen. I was shy and too nervous to put myself out there, considering I didn't know anyone. This resulted in me being almost completely alone for the rest of my junior year. I sat alone at lunch, I didn't talk to anyone in any of my classes, and I was failing most of them due to lack of motivation. It was a tough semester.

Still, during this time, I was exploring what styles I liked and disliked. I cut my hair to my shoulders, stopped wearing concealer, and applied very thick eyeliner–it was not a pretty picture. One day when I was driving with my dad, he turned to me and said, "I'm surprised you don't have your nose pierced or something." I had wanted my nose pierced for a while, but didn't bother asking my parents, because I assumed they'd immediately say no. But, after this, I convinced my dad and spent a month convincing my mom. My cousin Jazzy also wanted her nose pierced, so my mom said that if we did it together, then I would be allowed to, since that would make it sort of special. So sure enough, Jazzy and I got our noses pierced together at the end of May 2022 (it hurt really bad).

That summer, my mom started talking about an idea she had for a business she wanted to start called Everyday Adventures, bringing all kinds of adventures into your everyday life. I wasn't entirely sure what it would consist of in the beginning, but she's my mom, and I'll always be supportive of her ideas, so I went along with it. We started going to events, for the adventure of course, but also to promote her new idea. I must admit, I wasn't sure how successful it'd be in the long run, but every time we were on one of the adventures, my mom met someone new who was interested and just as excited about it as she was. She was always connecting with people, especially women. She connected with women so much that she decided to create other aspects of Everyday Adventures–the one that most of us know now is Everyday Girl Adventures. Every new place we went (and still go to) she introduced all kinds of different women, and even men, to Everyday Girl Adventures. So far, I don't think I've met a single person who isn't fascinated by my mom's adventure-driven personality and this idea that she's brought to them.

Following all of this, she started a networking group for women called MissFit Networking (where every "miss" fits), for women entrepreneurs who feel like they don't fit into a specific place. When she first started it, I thought it had nothing to do with me considering I'm in high school and not a grown woman or entrepreneur. I definitely felt out of place considering I was always the youngest one there. But, since her first MissFits event that September, I've been to (almost) every single one. Even though I may not be a woman entrepreneur, being surrounded by them from a young age has helped me understand that I'm not alone. I'm not the only one still figuring out what my dream is and what I want to do with my life. It also continues to inspire me, seeing women put their heart into something they are truly passionate about. And, surprisingly enough, I can actually relate to these women in some ways, despite the age difference. This past year has been eye-opening for me as a teen, still discovering who I am as a human being, and also constantly going on these adventures and attending events with my mom. And while I still don't know exactly what my passions are, I'm having fun going along on the adventure to find out.

The following story may contain material that is sensitive to some audiences. Enter this adventure at your own risk.

Adventures of a "Miss"terious Feast of the Senses

By Jennifer Harris

Her voice at my ear as she leaned in and told me to believe in myself. That I was worthy of love, worthy of prosperity, worthy of good things. Her breath caressed my neck, and she told me I was beautiful, and in that moment I was her most favorite thing about the event we were attending...

But I'm jumping ahead too far for you dear reader.. let me give you some background.

I'm Jennifer and I've been in the kink/BDSM scene actively for the last several years. I went to my first club experience in

January of 2019 to get out of my rut. I had been in a self-imposed celibacy for a year after a break up, and I decided I couldn't take it anymore. That first night, stations of different kinks were set up so you could experience a mini version of a scene. That night I tried a couple of things and fell in love with sensation play.

Sensation play is a very broad term and can incorporate a lot of various techniques. However, for me, it's mostly about how objects feel when being used on skin. Many people use everyday things that can be found around the house and then sprinkle in things that are more kink related. For this station, the demonstrator had a wide range of objects, but what I loved the most wound up being simple shower loofah gloves. I was dumbfounded when I discovered that!

The next day, I went on Amazon and placed an order for the most textured looking loofah gloves I could find and a pair of rabbit fur fingerless mittens. Once received, every time I went to my local club, I would ask people if they had experienced sensation play. Before long I hooked up with a woman who mentored me. Soon I was doing multiple scenes per night when attending a play party and built a reputation for my talent.

During this experience, I realized how much touch meant to me. Growing up I didn't get hugged much by family or friends. And, sadly, as an adult it has been the same. I unfortunately didn't know how to change that, because I wasn't sure how to go about it. Doing sensation play gave me an 'in', and I took it with both hands and allowed myself to grow. However being in control 90% of the time meant that I didn't personally receive any touch back. I simply gave, which is glorious, but different.

Fast forward to 2022 where I decided that I wanted to try something new. I was attending a kink conference on my own and hadn't talked to anyone about actually doing a scene, so I decided to try out doing a solo scene with audience participation on the last night of the conference. I had someone write out things attendees could do.

Waiting for the dungeon space to open, I was dressed in a mesh crop top and skirt. People could see the writing and started asking me about it. I explained that these were things

I'd love for people to do while I was positioned in a chair, blindfolded under a spot light in the space. Their eyes lit up, and they were super excited to participate and encourage others to do so as well. I started to fill with nervous joy at the thought of how this would play out.

I entered the dungeon, pulled a chair over, and found my spot. I undressed, placed my water bottle under my seat within easy reach, slipped on the blind fold, and sat facing the doors.

Soon other people poured in and found places to play or watch. I listened to conversations happening around me, the sound of impact tools being used, rope being slid over skin and then on the metal rig... and then I felt someone's hand on me, running their nails across my skin lightly. Their body gently pressed into mine as they breathed close to my ear. A giant smile spread across my face, and my skin danced in bliss. Time passed and the flow of voices, bodies, and energy wrapped itself around me in a beautiful cocoon of pleasure. It was glorious.

The woman from the start of this story came in, flowing affirmations over me. Her words, coupled with the other senses being worked on, had me filled up with such abundant joy and gratitude that I wanted to raise my hands and scream in happiness. I felt radiant. But I hesitated, because what if people thought that was weird? What if people stopped interacting with me if I did that? All the 'what if's' bogged down my brain.

Finally, I said fuck it, because who the hell cares? Even if any of that happened, it didn't matter. So I raised my hands and yelled at the top of my lungs–my voice flowing out the joy I was being filled with. As my hands came back down, I began to cry–tears filled with emotional release as well as any negativity I had been holding onto.

People didn't think I was weird, and the interactions didn't stop. They actually continued on for a couple more hours with me shifting directions on the chair when there was a lull. Only one time was there a bit of an energy weirdness, and had it not gone quite right I would have used my voice to ask the person to stop.

The night ended with me riding a high, knowing that not only did I do something new for myself that I will always remember, but that I was filled with words of encouragement, love, joy, passion and prosperity. I'm sure I gave inspiration to others to try something new.

I love new experiences that test my ideas, limits, and ways I can make my life better. I encourage you to think outside your box and try something new without overthinking it. You might find you have a new passion you can incorporate into your own life.

Adventures are not just for girls. We invite you to take a sneak peak into the next series of relatable stories told by everyday guys.

Adventures of a
"Mis"-ter's Late Revelation

By Bill Baxter

One autumn day, on October 11, 1954; in Fullerton, California, a young woman, Enid Baxter was giving birth to her second son, as Jack Baxter, the father, anxiously awaited. Dr. Neslund was delivering the child, who was coming in between ten and eleven pounds. That baby was me–William Edwin Baxter.

My mother was small, and since I was such an enormous baby, I got stuck in childbirth. Dr. Neslund had to make a split decision as to whether to deliver me by C-section or to use a pair of forceps (which are tongs used to pull out a baby who is stuck in childbirth). Dr. Neslund made the wrong decision and grabbed a pair of forceps, squeezed me just beneath my head, and began to twist and pull me out by force. As I was pulled out of my mother's womb into the world, irreparable damage was done to my central nervous system. I was born developmentally disabled, with special needs. Dr. Neslund looked at my father and apologized for what happened as he said, "*I'm sorry. I should have taken him by C-section.*" The thing is, in 1954, physicians were a lot more apprehensive about performing C-sections.

My mother felt awfully bad about what had happened to me during my childbirth and resolved to "mainstream" me into society as much as she could possibly do. My parents even hid my being a forceps baby from me for most of my life so that I could pursue a normal life like others my age. They even destroyed all the documents proving that it happened.

There were a couple of ailments which also accompanied my life: Tourette's Syndrome and Bi-polar Disorder. During my early years, neither had yet come into the medical limelight in society and were a long way off from doing so. My brother, Jeff Baxter, knew from our childhood that I had special needs, but I didn't find out until just shy of my 56th birthday. My mother passed away in April 2009. I was kept in the dark until slightly over a year later when my father and I moved to Colorado Springs, Colorado to be closer to Jeff, who was a Presbyterian Minister there. One day my father and my brother finally revealed to me that I was born a forceps baby and was developmentally disabled.

About 52 years ago, right around the time I was in middle school, my mother did make known to me that there was some slight brain damage and that I was hyperactive, but for the longest time, I believed for the most-part that I was as normal as everyone else. I didn't realize the full gist of my disability until later on, but a lot of my classmates in elementary and middle school knew I wasn't normal. They, in fact, resented me and felt I didn't belong with them. From the 6th grade on up to being a freshman in high school, I was treated as a social outcast. I couldn't understand why. The more kids my age made me feel unwelcome and bad about myself, the harder I would strive to be successful in everything I did and prove them wrong. My mother had taken a gamble trying to keep me in normal social and educational settings. Being a social outcast, for a reason I did not yet understand, took an emotional toll on me, but it paid off in the long haul. Little did I know, my life was about to change for the better.

In the year 1971, I was living in Fair Oaks, California (outside Sacramento), and my family was attending the First Presbyterian Church. I was a member of a high school fellowship group and accepted Jesus Christ as my Lord and Savior. When we moved to the

Washington, D.C. area, I began attending Thomas S. Wootton High School in Rockville, Maryland. I was in Special Ed part-time, but the rest of the time I was in regular classes. I made it a point to make the best of my new school and get involved. I served as Team Manager for Varsity Football, Varsity Wrestling, and the Track Squad. The coaches liked me and the work I did, and so the athletes (some of them among the most popular kids in school) looked up to these coaches, and befriended me as well. All of a sudden, I was no longer an outcast.

Most kids my age who also had special needs were in special education classes (they were called EMR classes back then) for entire school years. However, I had only been in special education during my 2nd and 3rd grade years, from 1963-65, and part time during my sophomore and junior years. The rest of the time I was in regular classes like everyone else. Not knowing I was developmentally disabled while in these normal classes gave me an edge in life to be more successful in mainstream settings. This helped me to go above and beyond my disabilities and be an inspiration to a lot of people. I was even voted *"The Most Improved Student"* in my high school class of 1974.

Despite this, high school advisors tried to convince my mother to tell me that I should not attend college because they felt I was not college material. My mother, who wanted me to have a chance at a normal, productive life replied: "*I will not! If my son wants to attend college, I am going to let him try.*" I was on a roll at Thomas S. Wootton High School, so I made up my mind–I was going to give college a try. I graduated from Ohlone College in Fremont, California with an Associate of Arts Degree in June 1977 and from California State University East Bay with a Bachelor of Science Degree in August 1979.

I continued to strive for success after college, while living in Orange County, California. I excelled in singing during the 1980's and became an accomplished member of Toastmasters International during the 1990's. I received the Distinguished Toastmaster Award in February 1996–their highest achievement level.

I still needed to learn and embrace who I really was, as a man who had been developmentally disabled and part of the special needs population since birth. I first began to see that I was a person with disabilities when I was officially diagnosed with Tourette's Syndrome in 1996. For almost 15 years, I believed that was the extent of my disabilities, until the late revelation from my brother and father in 2011. A year later, a psychologist also diagnosed me with Bi-polar

Disorder. I was then in total touch with who I really was.

As it turns out, Colorado Springs is a big city oasis for the special needs minority group. I started to become more involved with people who have special needs. I found a full-time job working for Service Source, Inc. Service Source is a nationwide non-profit company that hires people with disabilities to work at federal government installations as civilian contract workers. In Colorado Springs they hire people with special needs to work at the U.S Army post at Fort Carson, so I worked there in the various dining facilities as "kitchen police" and doing janitorial work for a little over 10 years. Helping these young men and women who were putting their lives on the line for our freedom gave me great satisfaction during my time with Service Source, Inc. I retired on October 11, 2020 but stayed on at Fort Carson part-time for two years. On October 8, 2022, I fully retired. I am also a member of The Arc of the Pikes Peak Region, which helps people with developmental disabilities.

Before my "Late Revelation" of being a forceps baby and developmentally disabled, I was accomplishing great things people like me aren't expected to achieve. In doing so, I was inspiring a whole lot of people. I realized I needed to continue doing so by going above and beyond my disabilities now that I am in total touch with who I really am and involved in the local special needs community. Therefore, I have continued to be involved with Toastmasters International here in Colorado Springs, and in recent years, I have become a published children's author and holiday recorded artist.

My family had kept quite a secret from me for most of my life, even past the day when my mother went to be with the Lord. They all, and particularly my mother, wanted me to have as close to a normal life as possible. However, there were things my parents let my brother, Jeff, do that I could not because of my disabilities. Since I was in the dark about my situation, this painted a false picture of my parents giving my brother special treatment over me, which I now know wasn't the case. Whenever I accused them of this, rather than my parents coming clean on who and what I was, I was met with harsh corporal punishment. That was sufficient grounds for me being taken away from my parents, but I am glad that never happened.

When I think back on my story, I ask myself, what would have happened if my family hadn't gone through these lengths to keep this secret from me, and what if I hadn't been mainstreamed? I am an old man now. I can look back on my life to see how successful my life has been for a man with disabilities and how I have made a difference. If this had happened the opposite way–if I had known I was developmentally disabled and treated as such–I feel my life would not have been nearly as successful or that I would have made as big of a difference. I wouldn't have inspired as many people.

This "Late Revelation" all goes back to Ecclesiastes 3:11: *"He hath made everything beautiful in His time."* And that is exactly what God has done in my life.

Meet the Authors

Jaime Obertubbesing

Hi, I'm Jaime! My two cats, Sterling and Snowflake, and I live in Colorado Springs, where I have been teaching for the past nine years. I'm an elementary school teacher by day, retail manager by night, and up for any adventure in between!

I got into teaching because I love the energy, passion, and sense of wonder that children possess. There is something special about witnessing that spark in a child's eyes when a concept finally clicks. I also admire how children feel each moment and don't hold back. I've always wondered at what point we lose that innocence and become so self-aware, so I try to live life through a child's eyes–enjoying each moment for what it is and the memories that come along with them.

I am known for taking pictures of everything–capturing a moment is so incredibly valuable to me. I also enjoy creative writing. Consequently, it has always been a dream of mine to dip my toes in journalism and editing. One day, I would love to make a career out of that passion.

Despite my crazy schedule, I always make time for plenty of fun. I spend my weekends enjoying live music, dancing, soaking up the sunshine as much as possible, and hanging out with friends and family. To me, it never matters what I am doing–it is enjoying the company I'm sharing the experience with. And I'm always up for a new adventure. After all, life is too short to be anything but happy.

Tiffany McKee

Hi, I'm Tiffany! My life is chaos, hence me thriving in it. I have two kids, the cutest dogs in the world (I'll die on that hill), and a ridiculous make-up obsession–whether or not I have my eyebrows on is a gauge for everyone to know how I'm feeling. I fully stand that 4am is the winner's hour–if you're not up by seven getting shit done, what are you even doing? And I believe being a good human comes at no cost.

I was born and raised in Fontana, California (the Inland Empire). When I was 15, I ran my aunt's Fluff and Fold Laundry Service and was also her booking agent for limo runs. That's where I found my love of customer engagement. I graduated high school at 16, and that passion turned into my current 18 year career in food/retail management.

When I'm not at work, I enjoy reading, shopping, and binge watching murder shows. My ultimate goal is to live a comfortable, humble life, making a good living to give my kids everything they deserve—what I never had growing up. One day you'll find me soaking up the sun at a beach-front house in Santa Barbara, California. Remember, you live every day, but only die once.

Romina Cela

My name is Romina. The things that define me are: I'm a mom of three kids: two boys and one girl. I can't function without coffee (I actually missed a plane once because I was getting my coffee). I am a wine snob (hard not to be when Italians taught you how to taste wine) and I love to sip on neat whiskey (I started drinking hard liquor when I was 16). I have lived in five different countries on two different continents, grew up in communism, speak three languages fluently, and traveled in more countries than I can count. I love good food, travel, and intelligent conversations, my family and friends, and I'm always up for a good time!

My typical day is pretty normal. I work from home, so it's almost like I roll from one job to the other, (professional by day, homemaker by night). Then it's the gym (if I can manage), sleep, get up, and repeat. I live in an area (D.C.), where there is a lot to do with my 4-year-old, so we take advantage of the weekends and try to do as much as possible: museums, parks, aquariums, and so forth. My family lives in Europe so I spend a lot of time on the phone as well with them.

Kam Fletcher

Hi, I'm Kam! I have a new fun business teaching everyone from 3 to 93 years old how to make sourdough bread. I'm known as the Haphazard Sourdough Baker because I've made every mistake in the world and my bread still turns out. Check me out on Facebook and Instagram: @haphazard.sourdough.baker

Sheridan West

Hi, I'm Sheridan! I'm a call center trainer by day and an entrepreneur by night. I spend most of my days working hard, but I love to sprinkle in fun as well! I love to try new things, go on unique adventures, and meet new people.

Kay Rowe

Hi, I'm Kay! I reside in Colorado Springs, CO, surrounded by family, friends and breath-taking mountain trails. In addition to being an author and writing coach, I am a realtor (licensed in NE and CO) and a mediator. My passion to help people enjoy a higher quality of life is what drives me in everything that I do.

Holly Melby

Hi, I'm Holly! I have been married to my husband Jeff for 24 years and together we are raising three kids, aged 14, 13, and 7. After serving my family as a stay-at-home mom for several years, I am now pursuing a long-time dream of writing. I am the author of everything from children's books, to social media content, to a blog. But my real passion is simply stringing words together with the intention of empowering others.

Lang Netzler

Lang Netzler earned a Bachelors in Biology, with emphasis in Biotechnology/ Biochemistry. For her undergraduate thesis, she studied epigenetics by modifying gene activity of yeast cells. She continued her education at the Advanced Therapy Institute of Touch, and became certified in Integrative Meridian Therapy and Somatic Trauma Release Therapy. She opened a private practice called C.H.A. Family Wellness.

She believes in working with the body as a whole organism, rather than compartmentalizing it into separate systems. She advanced from modifying yeast cells to taking her clients on a healing journey to restore their nervous system health; she helps clients' bodies switch from being stuck in flight-or-fight response to the rest-and-digest mode, where the body heals. She transforms personal and physical injuries and creates closures for emotional injuries.

She is compassionate and trauma-informed. As a result, her clients' health are balanced physically, mentally, emotionally, and spiritually.

Chhiv "Lang" Netzler is married to Henry Netzler. They are blessed with a beautiful daughter, named Ava. They love going out to eat, especially at their own neighborhood bar & restaurant named Back on the Boulevard. They love taking family vacations: weekend staycations, Salida hot springs, Aspen with friends, Hawaii, and anywhere with a sitting area, resting, digesting, and watching the sunset.

Ashley Huyck

Hi, I am Ashley; online course creator, formerly a teacher, turned professional encourager. I am mama to the kindest 5-year-old girl who loves all things Halloween and animals.

My day to day adventure goes a little something like this... Wake up early and make a cup of coffee and get my mini me to school. Then, work in a dental office and do all things insurance and patient coordination. Most afternoons I go to the gym and lift weights–I am training to be a powerlifter. After almost killing myself there, I scoop up my mini me, and we cook dinner together and I do the mom thang. I usually end up falling asleep putting my mini to bed.

In my free time I enjoy creating, making jewelry, painting, and trying new crafts. Living in Colorado, I enjoy walks while listening to podcasts and being out in the sunshine!

Taunya Kepple

Hi, I'm Taunya! I'm a mom of two boys, 12 and 18 years old, and a 4-year-old golden retriever. I'm engaged and in my 23rd year of my career as an engineering manager. I think I've only stayed home in pajamas four times in the past 30 years, so let's just say I keep busy!

Teresa Morey

My name is Teresa. I grew up in Florida, where I first met my husband. Military life first took us to England, where we shared many adventures traveling as much as we could throughout Europe. Because there is so much to see and do in Europe, we celebrated our first anniversary in Paris, France and our second in Edinburgh, Scotland. We also traveled to Germany, Amsterdam, and Italy in between. This amazing opportunity taught me to try new experiences and cultures, and I made many lasting friendships along the way.

After Europe, we got stationed in a remote area in New Mexico–such a drastic change! But I learned that no matter where you live, as long as you have friends, you can create your own adventures! We have since retired from military life and have settled down to raise our son in Colorado Springs, CO.

Maggie Rasch

My name is Maggie. I am the proud mother of ten children. My children are my pride and joy, and I live vicariously through their triumphs and successes.

An adventurous spirit resides within my soul, and I am a true travel enthusiast. From road trips to traveling through Europe with my daughters, I embrace the thrill of new experiences. I have embarked on numerous family adventures over the years, creating cherished memories that will last a lifetime.

Reese Walton

My name is Reese. I have a passion for psychology and a deep interest in understanding the inner workings of the human mind. I enjoy exploring different theories and analyzing how and why people think and behave the way they do. In my free time, I enjoy reading articles on psychology or watching documentaries that delve into the subject.

I have an eye for photography and capturing the beauty in everyday moments. In my free time, I also enjoy writing short stories and essays that explore different aspects of life and the world. I love all animals, especially horses, and of course, my dog, Abbey.

Jennifer Harris

I'm Jennifer, and I'm a creative entrepreneur. My main work passion is capturing intimate portraits of people of all genders and helping them see how glorious they truly are. I promote body and sexy positivity with an open mindset and love to help educate people on various aspects of this perspective.

One of my big "whys" in life, besides helping others, is to travel. I find delight in seeing new places, meeting new people, and experiencing new things.

William Baxter

I'm William Baxter, but I go by Bill. I lived most of my life in the Anaheim/Orange County Area until moving to Colorado Springs, Colorado in 2010. There I worked ten years for Service Source Inc., which is an organization that hires people with disabilities as civilian contract workers in the U.S. Army Post at Fort Carson, CO. I am now retired and have become a published children's author and holiday recorded artist. I am also a season ticket holder for the Colorado Springs Switchbacks soccer team (USL) and have sung the National Anthem for them a few times.

I have been disabled from birth but have gone through life not letting this defeat me. Instead, I have constantly tried to go above and beyond my disabilities to accomplish great things and inspire a lot of people through my resilience.

This is not where the adventures end. It's where they begin….

Join us in the fun! If you'd like to be a part of an upcoming adventure series, please submit your own everyday adventure story to everydayadventures1111@gmail.com!